Connecting the cross and the reasons – not least the implic. evangelism. Tim Chester has d just two key biblical themes but so in a warm and accessible way. of Jesus the king who suffered.

CW00336439

Graham Beynon
Pastor, Grace Church Cambridge
and Director of Independent Ministry Training, Oak Hill College, London

It is hard to imagine a more needed book today than Tim Chester's *Crown of Thorns*. By holding together things that should not be put asunder, especially the gospel of the cross with the gospel of the kingdom, he offers a needed corrective to some who would pit these themes against each other. Even more, he reminds us that the way of God's rule and reign is the way of King Jesus' dying and rising again. His crucifixion and resurrection serve as the basis of his removing the curse as far as it is found! What good news to our generation!

Sean Michael Lucas
Senior Minister, The First Presbyterian Church,
Hattiesburg, Mississippi

We have a tendency to divide the things that God has revealed to us as whole. We are often a reactionary church over-emphasizing one doctrine in an attempt to correct past missteps to the neglect of another doctrine. The cycle of action, reaction, and over-reaction spirals the church into a shallow and chaotic sea of empathetic theology. Sadly, we have even attempted to put the gospel of the kingdom against the gospel of the cross! Tim Chester is a faithful guide who shows how king Jesus reigns in his kingdom through the dark day on Golgotha. This book is an absolute gift for those who want a holistic discipleship that 'teaches them to obey everything I have commanded you' (Matt. 28:20).

Daniel Montgomery
Lead Pastor, Sojourn Community Church, Louisville, Kentucky
Founder, Sojourn Network
and author of *Faithmapping* and *PROOF*

Do I seek social justice or proclaim salvation? Are there Jesus Christians and Paul Christians? Is it narrative versus epistle? Must I choose kingdom or cross? Why does the attractive, contemporary call to crazy, whole-hearted, justice-seeking discipleship seem so passionately parable-and-narrative-flavoured while the declaration of salvation through Christ alone seem so narrowly propositional? Is it jungle versus zoo, menagerie versus museum, where the price of gospel clarity is cage, bar and glassy-eyed lifelessness?

Crown Of Thorns is a readable, relevant, important, biblically sharp consideration of the current kingdom versus cross dynamics which decide the foundations on which we end up building our life, ministry and discipleship. Tim Chester's conclusions lie not in a self-cancelling neutrality or a bland balancing act but in whole-hearted commitment to the Hero of apostolic teaching – Christ the Saving, Serving, Loving, Risen, Coming, Conquering King.

Colin Buchanan
Christian children's recording artist and author, Sydney, Australia

Crown of Thorns addresses one of the most common discussions in modern evangelicalism: the dichotomy between the "Cross Gospel" and the "Kingdom Gospel". Kingdom without Cross amounts to a mere human campaign which replaces personal salvation with social reform. On the other hand, preaching the Cross without the Kingdom can often ignore the Gospel's lifestyle challenge. Tim Chester skilfully integrates and weaves together the two dimensions of Cross and Kingdom towards a healthy, scriptural understanding of Christ's accomplishment. He shows that, as the Bible is properly comprehended, it is the Cross-shaped message of the atonement in the hands of Christ-shaped disciples that will bring about the reestablishment of God's ultimate rule.

Iver Martin
Principal, Edinburgh Theological Seminary, Edinburgh, Scotland

Crown of
Thorns

Connecting
Kingdom and Cross

Tim Chester

CHRISTIAN
FOCUS

Tim Chester is an author, pastor of The Crowded House, Sheffield and a leader of The Crowded House church planting network. He is married with two daughters.

Copyright © Tim Chester 2015

paperback ISBN: 978-1-78191-614-8
epub ISBN: 978-1-78191-617-9
mobi ISBN: 978-1-78191-618-6

10 9 8 7 6 5 4 3 2 1

Published in 2015
by
Christian Focus Publications Ltd,
Geanies House, Fearn,
Ross-shire, IV20 1TW, Scotland.
www.christianfocus.com
and
Porterbrook Network
215 Sharrow Vale Road
Sheffield, S11 8ZB
www.porterbrooknetwork.org

Cover design by Daniel van Straaten

Printed by
Bell and Bain, Glasgow

CONTENTS

'The Lord has established his sovereignty from a tree.'[1]
(St. Augustine)

---

1. Cited in Jeremy R. Treat, *The Crucified King: Atonement and Kingdom in Biblical and Systematic Theology,* (Zondervan, 2014), 29.

One

Two Gospels
and Two Missions?

There are two gospels within evangelical churches today. One gospel focuses on the kingdom of God – the good news that Christ has come to inaugurate God's reign and thereby put the world right. The other focuses on the cross – the good news that Christ died in our place so that all who trust in him might be forgiven.

Sometimes they present themselves as complementary accounts which reflect different aspects of the breadth of the biblical narrative. Sometimes they confront one another as competing versions of the true gospel. Some people hold one and not the other. Some try to balance both. Many acknowledge varying degrees of validity in the position of the other, but in practice emphasize one over the other.

My aim in this book is both to unite and divide. I want to unite those who are committed to the one gospel. I have tried to show that advocates of a kingdom-centred gospel and of a cross-centred gospel in fact have much in common.

But I also want to divide. I want to delineate the point where a different emphasis is in fact no gospel. There are ways of articulating the gospel that are wrong. And some of those ways omit elements which are so crucial that we are left with no gospel at all.

THE GOSPEL OF THE CROSS

In 1 Corinthians 2:1-2 Paul says: 'When I came to you, brothers, I did not come with eloquence or superior wisdom as I proclaimed to you the testimony about God. For I resolved to know nothing while I was with you except Jesus Christ and him crucified.' The gospel, it seems, that Paul preached was the good news of Jesus Christ and him crucified.

Later in the same letter to the Corinthians, Paul defines the gospel. He describes it as the gospel which the Corinthian church has received, on which its members have taken their stand and by which they are saved. This is what is of first importance (15:1-3). This is how he defines this gospel of first importance:

> That Christ died for our sins according to the Scriptures, that he was buried, that he was raised on the third day according to the Scriptures, and that he appeared to Peter, and then to the Twelve. After that, he appeared to more than five hundred of the brothers at the same time, most of whom are still living, though some have fallen asleep. Then he appeared to James, then to all the

apostles, and last of all he appeared to me also, as to one abnormally born (1 Cor. 15:3-8).

The gospel according to this summary consists of the events of the cross and resurrection. The death of Jesus is confirmed by his burial, and his resurrection is confirmed by his many post-resurrection appearances. But this gospel is also event-plus-interpretation and the interpretation is that Christ died 'for our sins according to the Scriptures'.

Paul makes a similar statement in Romans 4:25: '[Jesus our Lord] was delivered over to death for our sins and was raised to life for our justification.' Here we again meet the phrase 'for our sins'. We see again the centrality of the cross and resurrection. Through the cross and resurrection we have been justified. Paul goes on: 'Therefore, since we have been justified through faith, we have peace with God through our Lord Jesus Christ.'

This declaration brings to a climax the arguments in Romans 1–4. Paul has shown that all humanity has sinned and is now under judgment, Gentile and Jew alike (Romans 1:18–3:20). But God declares us righteous through faith in the redeeming work of Christ (3:21-24). In the Old Testament, God's righteous acts were his saving acts by which he vindicated his people in the face of their enemies. But our real enemy is God himself (Romans 5:10). God, however, has now vindicated us before God. In the face of the accusations that God himself makes against us, God declares us not guilty.

But God not only justifies us, he justifies himself. He justifies his actions in declaring us to be in the right when we are clearly in the wrong. God must declare us right and still act rightly. And that is why Jesus was crucified. God presented Jesus as a sacrifice 'to demonstrate his justice' (3:25-26). God demonstrates that he was just when he overlooked sin in the past (25b) and he demonstrates that he is just now when he justifies sinners in the present (26a). He did this through the sacrifice of Jesus Christ: 'God presented him as a sacrifice of atonement, through faith in his blood' (25a). When someone offered a sacrifice they symbolically transferred their sins onto the animal. Then what happened to the animal happened to their sins. The animal was a substitute for them. But when Jesus died on the cross it was not merely a symbol. Jesus took our sins on himself (Romans 8:1-4). Our sins were transferred on to him and so he died our death, taking our punishment.

The word translated 'sacrifice of atonement' is 'propitiation' which means 'turning aside wrath'. God's wrath in all its terrible destructive force is hurtling towards us like an on-coming train. On the cross Jesus interposed himself. He stood in the way of God's wrath. He took the full force of God's judgment against sin. He absorbed the power of hell. So now nothing of God's wrath gets through to us. In that act God justifies us, for our punishment is paid in full. And in that act God justifies himself, for there is punishment – the crime is not overlooked.

If God had simply declared us righteous, it would all be a legal fiction. It would be a case of 'Let's pretend'. 'Let's pretend people are right when really they are wrong.' We would be left with good reasons to suppose our salvation was a fiction, that we were not truly forgiven and not truly accepted by God. The verdict would be overturned on appeal. Because justice had not been done, the case would still be open. The threat of judgment would remain. But when God declares us right, even though we are wrong, he still acts rightly. Through the cross, we can be confident that we are right before him.

This courtroom, of course, is not simply a metaphor. A day is coming when that court will be convened. On the final day of judgment humanity will stand in the dock. God will wrap up history and call us all to account. He will present his case and pass judgment. Justification is a word about the future, about that future. Justification is a promise, an eschatological word. It is the assurance that when the courtroom drama reaches its climax with you standing in the dock before the Judge of all the world and your verdict is declared, you will, if you have put your faith in Christ, hear the words, 'Not guilty'.

This is the word of promise that comes in the gospel. The gospel is the promise of acquittal and the invitation to believe. This in essence is the gospel of the cross.

THE GOSPEL OF THE KINGDOM

Jesus began his ministry by declaring: 'The time has come. The kingdom of God is near. Repent and believe the good news!' (Mark 1:14-15). Jesus proclaims good news and the good news is that the kingdom of God is near.

Matthew uses the phrase 'the gospel' or 'good news of the kingdom' three times in his Gospel:

- Jesus went throughout Galilee, teaching in their synagogues, preaching *the good news of the kingdom*, and healing every disease and sickness among the people (Matt. 4:23).

- Jesus went through all the towns and villages, teaching in their synagogues, preaching *the good news of the kingdom* and healing every disease and sickness (Matt. 9:35).

- And *this gospel of the kingdom* will be preached in the
  whole world as a testimony to all nations, and then
  the end will come (Matt. 24:14).

Luke also refers to the gospel of the kingdom of God three
times in his Gospel plus one further occurrence in Acts:

- But [Jesus] said, 'I must preach *the good news of the
  kingdom of God* to the other towns also, because that
  is why I was sent' (Luke 4:43).

- After this, Jesus travelled about from one town
  and village to another, proclaiming *the good news
  of the kingdom of God*. The Twelve were with him
  (Luke 8:1).

- The Law and the Prophets were proclaimed until
  John. Since that time, *the good news of the kingdom
  of God* is being preached, and everyone is forcing his
  way into it (Luke 16:16).

- But when they believed Philip as he preached *the good
  news of the kingdom* of God and the name of Jesus
  Christ, they were baptised, both men and women
  (Acts 8:12).

The gospel that Jesus proclaimed was the gospel of the
kingdom.

A focus on the kingdom of God is in part the result
of a developing understanding of the kingdom of God
in New Testament theology over the past 150 years. The
nineteenth-century German theologian, Albrecht Ritschl,
conceived of the kingdom of God in ethical terms. The
kingdom of God, he believed, was an ethical programme
centred on love. Some took Ritschl's understanding and
applied it in individualistic terms, locating the kingdom
of God in a person's heart as a call to live in the light

of the fatherhood of God and the brotherhood of humanity. Others applied it in a corporate way as a social programme. This movement became known as the social gospel and was particularly associated with the American pastor Walter Rauschenbusch. The agenda of this gospel of the kingdom was to transform the social order around the themes of love and solidarity. Arguably it was an attempt to rework the kingdom of God in the image of Enlightenment values. It was strongest at the end of the nineteenth century when hopes for progress were high. The kingdom of God became a religious way of talking about the advance of Western civilisation. All of this was shattered by the horrors of the First World War. After that it became harder to conceive of the kingdom of God as gradually developing within human history.

In 1892 Johannes Weiss (who was the son-in-law of Ritschl) published *Jesus' Proclamation of the Kingdom of God.* Weiss rejected Ritschl's understanding. He emphasized the future apocalyptic character of the kingdom of God. The kingdom that Jesus preached, he argued, would involve a sudden work of God overturning the present order. Weiss' work sparked a storm within New Testament scholarship and ignited a huge amount of interest in the kingdom of God which rumbled on throughout the twentieth century. Weiss' ideas were picked up by Albert Schweitzer. Schweitzer saw the kingdom of God in terms of what he called 'consistent eschatology' or 'thorough-going eschatology'. In other words, far from seeing the kingdom as a gradually developing phenomenon within history, Jesus conceived of it as a decisive future divine intervention. Schweitzer thought Jesus expected the kingdom to come in the mission of the twelve described in Mark 6:7-13. Jesus sent them out not expecting to see them again. When he was proved mistaken, Jesus decided to stake all, forcing God's hand by precipitating his own death.

The British scholar C. H. Dodd reacted against Schweitzer, taking a completely opposite position. In his 1935 book *The Parables of the Kingdom* he spoke of 'realized eschatology'. He argued that the miracles of Jesus were presented as the evidence that the kingdom of God had *already* come with the arrival of Jesus. Since this coming clearly did not involve the end of history, the kingdom of God became in Dodd's thought an a-historical reality. History becomes the vehicle for the eternal. In a similar way, the German liberal scholar Rudolf Bultmann 'de-mythologized' the kingdom of God. Bultmann believed we should not take the biblical accounts of miracles literally. Instead, he saw them as pictures of transcendent truths. We should take them seriously, he argued, but for Bultmann this involved seeing beyond the myth of the miraculous to the truth the miracles encapsulated. We need to 'de-mythologize' them. In this vein Bultmann believed that the kingdom of God comes in moments of existential crisis in which eternity intersects with time as the word of God is proclaimed. He makes the kingdom of God a reality which transcends history.

More recently the consensus of New Testament scholarship has positioned itself between Schweitzer and Dodd, led by scholars such as W. G. Kümmel in his 1961 book, *Promise and Fulfilment*. The kingdom is recognised as being both present and future. It has come and is coming. It was inaugurated at the first coming of Jesus, but awaits its consummation when he returns. This position is often called 'inaugurated eschatology'. This is the position advocated by the evangelical scholar, George Eldon Ladd, and it is primarily following the lead of Ladd that evangelicals have joined the consensus of 'inaugurated eschatology'. Ladd's book, *Jesus and the Kingdom* (later republished as *The Presence of the Future*, 1974) has been particularly influential.

Interweaving with this debate about the timing of the kingdom has been a debate about its *nature*. The term 'kingdom' can be misleading as it implies in English a domain or realm over which a king rules. But the Greek word (*basileia*) can also mean the act of reigning. It could be translated 'rule', 'reign', 'government' or 'sovereignty'.

There is an important sense in which God currently rules over this world because he is sovereign. But Jesus speaks of the coming of God's kingdom. The term 'the coming of God's kingdom' therefore clearly means more than simply God's sovereign or providential rule. The kingship of God is disputed. At the Fall, humanity rejected God's rule. The kingdom of God is the reassertion of that rule.

But is that rule the realm over which God reigns or the act of reigning? If the kingdom is simply the realm over which God rules, then it must either be future or transcendent or individualistic since the world is clearly not currently the realm over which God rules in an undisputed way. If, however, the kingdom refers to the actions of God, then it becomes possible to speak of that activity within history. The kingdom can be seen as the dynamic activity of God in history.

As a result scholars tend to emphasize that the kingdom of God is the active reign of God. But we should not entirely discount the idea of realm. Jesus speaks of people 'entering' the kingdom and you cannot 'enter' an activity. So the kingdom of God is both the act of God reigning and the people over whom he thereby reigns.

The gospel of the kingdom which Jesus proclaimed is the good news that God's reign was coming. And God's reign means justice, peace and restoration. Jesus not only preached this message, he also embodied it in his life and ministry. His miracles are pictures of God's saving reign. And his welcome of the marginalized embodied the forgiveness of the kingdom.

The gospel of the kingdom also comes with a call to repentance. It is a call to turn from the violence and greed of this world and embrace the bounty and grace of God's kingdom. The gospel of the kingdom thereby creates the community of the kingdom. The community of Jesus becomes the place on earth in which the kingdom is taking shape. It becomes the place in which the future can be seen.

So the gospel of the kingdom is a message of future liberation. But the new regime has begun among Christ's community of the broken. The Christian community is both a sign and a promise of God's coming liberation. We are the presence of God's liberating kingdom in a broken world.

For now, we go on living under the old regimes of this world. But a new regime has begun. A revolution has taken place. The old ways of oppression are coming to an end. A new community with a new government has begun. It operates secretly in the midst of this world. It is a community that offers peace and justice. This is the good news of the kingdom.

I trust that I have presented these two gospels – the gospel of the cross and the gospel of the kingdom – in ways that I hope their advocates would recognize. I trust, too, that we can see that both have some *prima facie* biblical warrant. This is not a case of a straight black-and-white choice. Do we, then, need to balance an emphasis on the cross and an emphasis on the kingdom? My argument will be that it is not a case of needing to balance these two themes so much as to connect them. We need a co-ordinated gospel in which the cross is central to the gospel of the kingdom and the kingdom is central to the gospel of the cross.

This discussion matters because these competing emphases create contrasting approaches to discipleship and mission.

TWO GOSPELS AND TWO MISSIONS?

'Kingdom people', 'kingdom ministry', 'kingdom ethics', 'kingdom hopes', 'kingdom vision', 'kingdom agenda'. At some point in the last thirty years the word 'kingdom' became an adjective. It is not always clear what this adjective is supposed to do for the word it qualifies. Is it simply there to make it sound more exciting? Or does it designate some qualitative difference in what is being described? How is 'kingdom ministry' different from other ministries?

Advocates of the cross-centred gospel do the same thing albeit in code. They replace the adjective 'kingdom' with the adjective 'gospel'. 'Gospel people', 'gospel ministry', 'gospel ethics', 'gospel hopes', 'gospel vision', 'gospel agenda'. This has perhaps replaced the word 'evangelical', which used to do this job but which has grown too diffuse to demarcate what the term 'gospel' now demarcates. This is a kind of code language for people who want to make the cross central and affirm the centrality of God's inerrant word.

THE DEATH OF JESUS VERSUS THE LIFE OF JESUS

Many advocates of a kingdom-centred gospel talk about
the need to rediscover the life of Jesus and the example of
Jesus. Those who focus on the cross point out that around
a third of the material found in the Gospels describes the
passion of Jesus even though that adds up to just one week
in a three-year ministry. But that, of course, still leaves two-
thirds of the Gospels covering the life and teaching of Jesus.

EPISTLES VERSUS GOSPELS

Linked to the relative emphases on the life and death of
Jesus is the question of the emphasis placed on the Gospels
and the Epistles. Advocates of a kingdom-centred gospel
claim that modern evangelicalism is largely shaped by
the Epistles with insufficient attention being given to the
Gospels. This is Tom Wright's central claim in his book,
How God Became King. Wright says: 'This problem can be
summarized quite easily: *we have all forgotten what the four
gospels are about.*'[1] In particular he accuses evangelicals of
having assumed '"the gospel" is what you find in Paul's
letters, particularly in Romans and Galatians':

> This 'gospel' consists, normally, of a precise statement of
> what Jesus achieved in his saving death ('atonement')
> and a precise statement of how that achievement could
> be appropriated by the individual ('justification by faith').
> Atonement and justification were assumed to be at the
> heart of 'the gospel'. But 'the gospels' – Matthew, Mark,
> Luke and John – appear to have almost nothing to say
> about those subjects.[2]

---

1. Tom Wright, *How God Became King: Getting to the Heart of the Gospels*,
    (SPCK, 2012), ix.

2. ibid., 6; see also 23.

He then asks of the whole Western tradition: 'Have we even begun to hear what [the gospels] are saying, the whole message, which is so much greater than the sum of the small parts with which we are, on one level, so familiar? I don't think so.'[3]

PAUL VERSUS JESUS

This links to another debate within New Testament scholarship: the relationship between Jesus and Paul. Paul is sometimes described as the creator or founder of Christianity. What is implied in this assertion is that Paul reshaped the message of Jesus into something else, a philosophical system or an ecclesiastical institution, neither of which Jesus would have recognised. Evangelical advocates of the kingdom-centred gospel would not go this far. But listen to Michael Frost and Alan Hirsch:

> We evangelicals have for too long read Jesus through predominantly what have been called Pauline eyes … But by reading the gospel through the Epistles, a disturbing distortion develops. Effectively, the Gospels are not taken seriously as prescriptive texts for life, mission and discipleship.

They add that they 'affirm the Pauline view of Jesus'. But then they add: 'our perspectives of Jesus can be so weighted by and filtered through the Pauline interpretation of the Messiah that we are unable to see him without hearing the Pauline formulas in our heads.'[4]

---

3. ibid., 10. Wright shows the biblical connections between the cross and kingdom, but not the theological connections. As Treat says: 'Although N. T. Wright acknowledges [the substitutionary] aspect of Jesus' death, it plays little role in his telling of the story of redemption or in his way of connecting kingdom and cross.' Treat, *The Crucified King*, 132 fn. 9.

4. Michael Frost and Alan Hirsch, *The Shaping of Things To Come: Innovation*

THE SOTERIOLOGICAL VERSUS THE POLITICAL CAUSES
OF THE CROSS

Advocates of the kingdom-centred gospel must account
for the cross. Unavoidably the cross stands at the centre of
the Bible story. Why did Jesus die? There are two answers
to this question. Both are legitimate answers. There is the
answer from the human perspective: Jesus was killed because he and his message threatened the status and power
of the religious and political establishment. And there is
the answer from the divine perspective: Jesus was killed
in fulfilment of the divine plan of salvation to redeem his
people from sin and judgment through his atoning sacrifice in their place. Both these explanations are affirmed, for
example, in the prayer of the early church in Acts 4:27-28:
'Indeed Herod and Pontius Pilate met together with the
Gentiles and the people of Israel in this city to conspire
against your holy servant Jesus, whom you anointed. They
did what your power and will had decided beforehand
should happen.' The religious and political authorities did
not decide to kill Jesus because they wanted to fulfil the
divine plan of salvation! They had their own reasons for
killing Jesus. This is how Stanley Hauerwas accounts for
the crucifixion in his commentary on Matthew's Gospel:

 Jesus must be killed because Jesus is the Son of God. Jesus
 must be killed because Jesus has called into existence a
 new people who constitute a challenge to the world order
 based on lies and deceit. Jesus must be killed because
 he is a threat to all who rule in the name of safety and
 comfort. Jesus must be killed because we do not desire
 to have our deepest desires exposed. Jesus must be killed

and Mission for the 21st Century Church, (Hendrickson, 2003), 112-113.

because we do not believe in a God who creates us and who would come among us after our likeness.[5]

His death cannot be isolated from his life, because his death is the result of his life. He died because he had challenged the elites of Israel who used the law to protect themselves from the demands of God; he died because he challenged the pretentious power of Rome; and he died at the hands of the democratic will of the mob. He died because he at once challenged and offered an alternative to all forms of human polity based on the violence made inevitable by the denial of God.[6]

If both explanations for the death of Jesus matter, which matters more?

PROCLAMATION VERSUS SOCIAL ACTION[7]

The last fifty years have seen a renewed interest among evangelicals in social involvement. And the kingdom of God has been a key feature of this renewed emphasis.

This is because it allows people to put an individual's relationship with God – the traditional focus of evangelical soteriology – in a broader context of social transformation. In 1974 the Lausanne Congress brought together over 2,000 evangelicals from around the world to plan the evangelisation of the world. It was a ground-breaking event and the resulting Lausanne Covenant has become a significant statement of evangelical convictions and intent.

---

5.   Stanley Hauerwas, *Matthew: Brazos Theological Commentary on the Bible,* (Brazos, 2006), 235.

6.   ibid., 238.

7.   I have dealt with this issue in more detail in my book, *Good News to the Poor: Sharing the Gospel Through Social Involvement* (IVP/Crossway, 2004/2014).

During the Lausanne Congress, a group of participants drew up 'a response to Lausanne' which went further than the Covenant itself. This statement, entitled *Theology and Implications of Radical Discipleship*, defined the gospel as:

> God's Good News in Jesus Christ; it is Good News of the reign he proclaimed and embodies; of God's mission of love to restore the world to wholeness through the Cross of Christ and him alone; of his victory over the demonic powers of destruction and death; of his lordship over the entire universe; it is good news of a new creation, a new humanity, a new birth through him by his life-giving Spirit; of the gifts of the messianic reign contained in Jesus and mediated through him by the Spirit; of the charismatic community empowered to embody his reign of *shalom* here and now before the whole creation and make his Good News seen and known. It is Good News of liberation, of restoration, of wholeness, and of salvation that is personal, social, global and cosmic.

By defining the gospel in terms of the kingdom of God, they made social change not only part of mission, but part of the gospel. It is this factor, above all others, which perhaps distinguishes the social thinking of the radical evangelicals from that of the evangelical social activists of the nineteenth century.

By setting social action in the eschatological context of the kingdom of God, evangelicals, particularly those from this radical wing, have been able to shape a view of social action which is oriented towards change. By placing the kingdom at the heart of social action, they find a rationale for radical social change in line with the radical nature of the kingdom and its future. This is in contrast to those evangelicals who root social involvement in the doctrine of creation, and who thus tend to be politically conservative, seeking to preserve the creation order. Tito Paredes, for example, says: 'No truly adequate theology of social change can be stated without the hope of the coming of the kingdom of God, in which social transformation will reach its perfect fulfilment'.[8]

Advocates of social action have argued that it is inhibited by an other-worldliness stemming from an overly-future eschatology. When the eschatological blessings are seen predominantly in future terms, it is alleged, mission is seen primarily in terms of converting people in readiness for that future. Such an eschatology is portrayed as escapist, allowing Christians to side-line the radical demands of discipleship in the here and now. In contrast, when the kingdom of God is seen as already present, albeit with its consummation still future, then social action is no longer seen as a diversion from the central task of mission. God's reign has implications for all of life.

A GOSPEL FOR INDIVIDUALS VERSUS A GOSPEL FOR SOCIETY

Those who emphasize a cross-centred gospel often tend to focus on the conversion of individuals. A common image is that of a lifeboat rescuing individuals before it is too late. Salvation is conceived of in individualistic terms. In contrast those who focus on the kingdom of God see salvation in corporate or social terms. Salvation is the renewal of creation. Individuals are invited to be part of that renewal (or, in more extreme universalist positions, they are assumed to be part of it). Tim Keller comments:

---

8.   Tito Paredes, 'Culture and Social Change', *The Church in Response to Human Need,* eds. Vinay Samuel and Chris Sugden (Regnum, 1987), 62.

It should be acknowledged that the writers in this category continually speak of individual and corporate redemption in such phrases as 'not only individual salvation but also' or 'more than individual salvation' as a way of indicating that they are not denying or changing traditional evangelicalism but rather adding to it. But upon reflection, I find that the individual and corporate aspects of salvation, mission, and Christian living are often pitted against one another, and the individual aspect nearly eliminated.[9]

This is not simply a question of soteriology (whether salvation is individual or corporate), but also of eschatology. Some believe salvation will be corporate (the renewal of creation when Christ returns), but in the meantime it is individual. Our mission is to rescue individuals in readiness for that day. Advocates of kingdom-centred gospel tend to believe that the social aspects of salvation are taking shape in history (albeit in an imperfect way). Some see this as happening through the advance of social justice in society. Others see it as the church being formed into an alternative community under the reign of Christ which anticipates the renewal of all things.[10]

9.   Timothy Keller, *Centre Church: Doing Balanced, Gospel-Centred Ministry in Your City*, (Zondervan, 2012), 268.

10. I have dealt with this issue in more detail in the published version of my PhD thesis, *Mission and the Coming of God: Eschatology, the Trinity and Mission in the Theology of Jürgen Moltmann and Contemporary Evangelicalism* (Paternoster Theological Monographs, 2006).

Summary

Exclusive emphasis on the kingdom	Primary emphasis on the kingdom	Primary emphasis on the cross	Exclusive emphasis on the cross
Focus on Jesus as our model	Emphasis on Jesus as our model	Emphasis on Jesus as our Saviour	Focus on Jesus as our Saviour
Focus on the political causes of the cross (with a rejection of atonement)	Emphasis on the political causes of the cross (with a neglect of atonement)	The atonement is more important than the political causes of the cross	Focus on the atonement (with a rejection of any political implications)
Strong focus on social action (with a suspicion of proclamation)	Emphasis on social action (with a reactive approach to proclamation)	Proclamation is central (but there is a place for social action)	Proclamation is central (with a rejection of social action)
Salvation is the formation of God's kingdom in society	Salvation is the formation of God's kingdom in society plus personal conversion	Salvation is personal conversion plus the formation of God's kingdom in the church	Salvation is personal conversion

Some advocates of a cross-centred gospel have a truncated gospel which is so focused on me that it loses sight of God's glory and his purposes for the world. Meanwhile, some advocates of a kingdom-centred gospel truncate the gospel, denying the atoning work of Christ on the cross.

But for most participants in these debates it is not about what we affirm, but what we emphasize. Some speak explicitly of the need to re-balance evangelicalism.

Nevertheless what we emphasize is nearly as important as what we affirm, for what we emphasize is what shapes our churches and our mission.

By now readers may have guessed that essentially
I agree with both these 'gospels'. Yet, while I have undoubtedly caricatured both sides to a certain extent to
highlight the differences, there is clearly a divide. Is it a
question of balance?

Greg Gilbert describes two groups of believers (much
as I have done). Group A rightly argue that 'the gospel is
the good news that God is reconciling sinners to himself
through the substitutionary death of Jesus'. Group B
rightly argue that 'the gospel is the good news that God
is going to renew and remake the whole world through
Christ'. Gilbert believes these two groups talk past each
other. Group A believes Group B are missing the cross.
Group B believes Group A are too individualistic.

Gilbert's analysis is helpful. I think there is significant
truth in both sides of the divide. While sometimes the divide is real with some people advocating positions that are
really no gospel at all, more often the divide is more im-
aginary as people who broadly agree talk past each other.

Gilbert's solution is to speak of the gospel having two
foci – a wide focus and a narrow focus. There is only one
gospel, he insists. The narrow focus is on the incarnation,
cross, resurrection and reign of Christ. The wide focus
embraces all that Christ has thereby achieved.[11] He

---

11. Greg Gilbert, 'Addendum: The Gospel in Its Broader and Narrower
    Senses,' in Mark Dever, J. Ligon Duncan, R. Albert Mohler and C. J.
    Mahaney, *Proclaiming a Cross-Centred Theology* (Crossway, 2009),
    121-130. See also Kevin DeYoung and Greg Gilbert, *What is the
    Mission of the Church? Making Sense of Social Justice, Shalom and the Great
    Commission,* (Crossway, 2011), 91-113; Greg Gilbert, *What is the Gospel?*
    (Crossway, 2010); and D. A. Carson, 'What Is the Gospel? Revisited,' in
    Sam Storms and Justin Taylor, (Eds) *For the Fame of God's Name: Essays
    in Honour of John Piper,* (Crossway, 2010), 147-170.

concludes: 'There is only one gospel, not two … The gospel of the kingdom *necessarily* includes the gospel of the cross … More specifically, the gospel of the cross is the fountainhead of the gospel of the kingdom.' In other words, the cross is 'the means of entering [the kingdom]'.[12]

Like Gilbert, I want to insist that these two gospels are in fact one gospel: the good news of the King who dies for his people. Connecting the kingdom and the cross is not simply a question of emphasis nor of distinguishing act and implication. Nor is it simply about toggling the field of our telescope between broad and narrow. It is about understanding how the kingdom and the cross are integrally related.

To see how this works we need to set our discussions in the context of the wider Bible story.

---

12. DeYoung and Gilbert, *What is the Mission of the Church?*, 107-108, 112.

Two

THE KING WHO RESTORES: THE KINGDOM COMES AS PROMISED

Some advocates of a kingdom-centred approach make much of rediscovering the Jewishness of Jesus. Michael Frost and Alan Hirsch, for example, emphasize the need for us to go 'back to our roots' in 'the Hebrew spiritual tradition'. 'The Jewish heritage is the primordial matrix out of which Christianity was birthed, and which we would argue is the only matrix out of which it could be organically understood in its fulness.'[1]

What this return to the Jewish roots of Christianity actually means, however, seems to be a rather speculative reconstruction of first-century Hebrew spirituality. This

---

1.   Frost and Hirsch, *The Shaping of Things To Come*, 115-123, and Michael Frost and Alan Hirsch, *ReJesus: A Wild Messiah for a Missional Church*, (Peabody, MA/Sydney, Hendrickson/Strand, 2009).

then sets up some polarities between concrete (Hebrew and good) versus speculative thinking (Greek and bad) or between right action (Hebrew and good) and right thinking (Greek and bad).

I want to suggest the more constructive way of exploring the Jewishness of Jesus would be to see how he fulfils the promises of the Old Testament.

The Bible story begins: 'In the beginning God created the heavens and the earth. Now the earth was formless and empty, darkness was over the surface of the deep, and the Spirit of God was hovering over the waters. And God said, "Let there be light," and there was light' (Gen. 1:1-3). It is an assertion of the sovereignty of God. But this is not just any god. This is the Lord, the covenant God of Israel. The readers of Genesis did not first encounter God as the Creator. They knew him first as the God of the exodus who had delivered them from slavery and covenanted with them at Sinai. Genesis 1 is the claim that the God of Israel is in fact the Creator God and therefore the God of the world. It is a claim that Israel's God is King.

This claim is repeated throughout the Psalms, especially in Book Four of the Psalms (Pss. 90–106). These Psalms begin in Psalm 90 with a prayer of Moses, and together they seem to reflect the claim of the Pentateuch that the Lord is king. Again and again they assert that God reigns and that his reign is universal, extending even to 'distant shores'. Moreover, often this claim is linked to God's work in creation.

Before the mountains were born
    or you brought forth the earth and the world,
    from everlasting to everlasting you are God
(Ps. 90:2)

The LORD reigns, he is robed in majesty;
>   the LORD is robed in majesty and is armed
>   with strength.
>   Indeed, the world is established, firm and secure.
Your throne was established long ago;
>   you are from all eternity (Ps. 93:1-2).

For the LORD is the great God,
>   the great King above all gods.
In his hand are the depths of the earth,
>   and the mountain peaks belong to him.
The sea is his, for he made it,
>   and his hands formed the dry land.
Come, let us bow down in worship,
>   let us kneel before the LORD our Maker (Ps. 95:3-6).

For great is the LORD and most worthy of praise;
>   he is to be feared above all gods.
For all the gods of the nations are idols,
>   but the LORD made the heavens ...
Say among the nations, 'The LORD reigns.'
>   The world is firmly established, it cannot be moved;
>   he will judge the peoples with equity
(Ps. 96:4-5, 10).

The LORD reigns, let the earth be glad;
>   let the distant shores rejoice ...
The heavens proclaim his righteousness,
>   and all the peoples see his glory.
All who worship images are put to shame,
>   those who boast in idols – worship him,
>   all you gods! (Ps. 97:1, 6-7).

The LORD reigns,
>   let the nations tremble;
he sits enthroned between the cherubim,
>   let the earth shake (Ps. 99:1).

My days are like the evening shadow;
> I wither away like grass.
But you, O Lord, sit enthroned for ever;
> your renown endures through all generations …
In the beginning you laid the foundations of the earth,
> and the heavens are the work of your hands.
They will perish, but you remain;
> they will all wear out like a garment.
Like clothing you will change them
> and they will be discarded.
But you remain the same,
> and your years will never end
(Ps. 102:11-12, 25-27).

The Lord has established his throne in heaven,
> and his kingdom rules over all (Ps. 103:19).

Genesis 1 not only asserts that God reigns, but also that humanity reigns. God places Adam and Eve in the garden to rule over creation under God's rule: 'Rule over the fish of the sea and the birds of the air and over every living creature that moves on the ground' (Gen. 1:28).

God's rule is a rule of blessing and prosperity, peace and freedom. God places humanity in a garden, protecting and providing for them in a home. In Babylonian mythology humanity is made by the gods to service their needs by bringing them food. But the creation of humanity in the Genesis account ends with God serving the needs of humanity and inviting them to eat from any of the trees (with just one exception).

The coming of God's kingdom cannot mean that God starts reigning. He already reigns.

But his kingdom has been rejected by humanity. The Serpent portrays God's rule as tyrannical: '"You will not surely die," the Serpent said to the woman. "For God knows that when you eat of it your eyes will be opened, and you will be like God, knowing good and evil'" (Gen. 3:4-5). Adam and Eve reject God's rule because they believe this lie. From that point onwards humanity has believed that God is holding us back, preventing us being like God. The irony is that humanity was already 'like God'. In Genesis 1:26 God says: 'Let us make mankind in our image, in our likeness.' We think we will be more free without God. But we end up enslaved by sin.

The Bible is the story of God re-establishing his rule – his rule that brings life, salvation, peace and justice. But all the time we are hostile to God's rule because we think it will tyrannize us.

Not only does the Serpent persuade humanity to reject God's rule, he also redefines the whole notion of rule. The rejection of God's rule radically affects humanity's rule over creation. While God's rule was a rule of love, peace, freedom, blessing and life, the Serpent portrays it as oppressive and we have modelled human rule in the image of the Serpent's lie. So humanity's rule becomes oppressive. We rule over creation not as God rules – in a way that brings blessing, freedom and life. We rule in the image of Satan's lie. We tyrannize the earth. We pollute and destroy.

At the same time as we are exploiting creation, we are being ruled by creation. The order of creation is reversed. Humanity was to rule over the animals, but in Genesis 3 the Serpent rules over humanity. This is what is happening, for example, in drug misuse. Instead of ruling over the plants, we are ruled by the hop or the poppy.

In Genesis 12 God promises Abraham 'a nation' – a word which suggests a political entity ruled over by a king. God says to Abraham: 'I will make nations of you, and kings will come from you' (Gen. 17:6). This promise of kings anticipates the promise to David. But before David, there are only hints at the central role of God's king.

What we see instead is God himself liberating his people from the slavery of the rule of Pharaoh. God rescues his people through the exodus and brings them to Mount Sinai. There God enters into a covenant with Israel which constitutes them as his people and re-establishes his life-giving reign over them.

Believing the lie of Satan that God's rule is tyrannical, we often think of God's law as restrictive. But the psalmists had a very different perspective: 'Your law is my delight.' 'Oh, how I love your law!' (Ps. 119:77, 97). God's rule brings life, blessing, peace and justice. God rules through his word. The law of Moses is the word by which he would rule Israel – the rule which brings life, blessing, peace and justice. Israel had been liberated from the oppressive rule of Pharaoh. Now they were to live a way of complete contrast – a way of liberation. To the extent that Israel lives in obedience to the law given through Moses, they will demonstrate the goodness of God and his reign:

Observe [these decrees and laws] carefully, for this will show your wisdom and understanding to the nations, who will hear about all these decrees and say, 'Surely this great nation is a wise and understanding people.' What other nation is so great as to have their gods near them the way the Lord our God is near us whenever we pray to him? And what other nation is so great as to have such righteous decrees and laws as this body of laws I am setting before you today? (Deut. 4:6-8).

When Israel began life in the promised land it was ruled directly by God through his word. But time and again the people did not walk in the way of obedience to the LORD, so God judged them by handing them over to the surrounding nations. When Israel cried out in repentance he sent the judges to rescue them and then to rule over them.

The LORD was with the judges: 'Whenever the Lord raised up a judge for them, he was with the judge and saved them out of the hands of their enemies' (Judg. 2:18). Few of the judges are conventional heroes. Most are deeply flawed characters. The point is that behind them all is God. He is the true Judge and the true King. In Judges 11:27 Jephthah speaks of 'the LORD, the Judge'. Because the judges were raised up by God, there is no succession. There was no succession because God himself is the true king. The only attempt at succession is the story of Abimelech and this ends in tragedy, if not farce. Gibeon is offered the throne but refuses (Judg. 8:22-23), but he names his son 'Abimelech' which means 'son of the king' (Judg. 8:31). Abimelech attempts to take the throne, but what he creates is civil war in which he is killed by a millstone thrown from the tower by a woman (Judg. 9).

The closing line of the book of Judges is: 'In those days Israel had no king; everyone did as he saw fit' (Judg. 21:25). It is true that Israel had no king, but Israel had no human king because they had a divine King. The problem is that, as was the case in Eden and as has been the case throughout history, instead of acknowledging the kingship of God, 'everyone did as he saw fit'.

In 1 Samuel 7:15-16 Samuel is described as a judge. Samuel is the last true judge. The problem is that he

attempts succession, appointing his sons as judges. But
they are not raised up by God and they are not suited to
the role:

> When Samuel grew old, he appointed his sons as judges
> for Israel. The name of his firstborn was Joel and the name
> of his second was Abijah, and they served at Beersheba.
> But his sons did not walk in his ways. They turned aside
> after dishonest gain and accepted bribes and perverted
> justice (1 Sam. 8:1-3).

It is perhaps not surprising, then, when the people ask
Samuel for a king: 'So all the elders of Israel gathered
together and came to Samuel at Ramah. They said to him,
"You are old, and your sons do not walk in your ways; now
appoint a king to lead us, such as all the other nations
have"' (1 Sam. 8:4-5). In Deuteronomy 17, Moses had
described how kingship was to function in Israel. So a
request for a human king was not intrinsically wrong. But
for Israel this was a rejection of their identity as God's
people. They want a king 'like the nations'. It is also a
rejection of God's identity. They will not acknowledge the
kingship of God (1 Sam. 8:7-8).

Nevertheless God graciously gives the king they want.
Samuel anoints Saul as the first king of Israel. Saul's name
means 'asked for'. Saul is the king the people asked for.
But Saul does not rule under the rule of God. So he is
rejected as king. Instead Samuel anoints David. David is
God's choice.

David is anointed as the next king. The word 'christ'
in Greek or 'messiah' in Hebrew means 'anointed one'.
Israelite kings were not crowned, but anointed with oil.
So 'the christ' is God's anointed King. David is, in a very

real sense, the christ. He is God's anointed king at that time. God makes a covenant with David, promising his descendants an everlasting kingdom (2 Sam. 7). The christ will always rule over God's people.

A generation later the kingdom of Israel divides into two: the ten northern tribes form the kingdom of Israel while the two southern tribes form the kingdom of Judah under the Davidic dynasty. In the north there is a succession of coups. But in the south God maintains the Davidic line on the throne, not because the Davidic kings are more worthy, but in faithfulness to his covenant with David.

Nevertheless both halves of the kingdom end in disaster. The kings fail to reign under God and lead the people in his ways. The northern kingdom ends in destruction at the hands of the Assyrians. The southern kingdom ends up in exile in Babylon.

GOD WILL RESTORE HIS REIGN THROUGH HIS COMING KING

Out of the ruins of the kingdom the prophets bring a word of hope. In a variety of ways God promises the coming of his reign. He promises to restore Israel and make her pre-eminent among the nations. He promises that he will come in judgment against Israel's enemies. He speaks of 'a day of the Lord' in which evil will be judged and God's name will be vindicated.

Alongside these promises of a new kingdom, God promises a new king. He will raise up a new David who will re-establish God's rule over his people. And he will rule not only over Israel, but over all nations.

For to us a child is born, to us a son is given,
    and the government will be on his shoulders.
And he will be called Wonderful Counsellor,
    Mighty God, Everlasting Father, Prince of Peace.
Of the increase of his government and peace
    there will be no end.
He will reign on David's throne
    and over his kingdom,
establishing and upholding it with justice
    and righteousness from that time on and for ever.
The zeal of the LORD Almighty will accomplish this
(Isa. 9:6-7).

In Ezekiel 34, God denounces the shepherds (the leaders) of Israel. Instead he promises to send a new David – the great shepherd king – gather his flock and reign over them: 'I will place over them one shepherd, my servant David, and he will tend them; he will tend them and be their shepherd. I the Lord will be their God, and my servant David will be prince among them. I the Lord have spoken' (Ezek. 34:23-34).

But there is another side to the expectation of the coming kingdom. Isaiah speaks of 'the Servant of the LORD'. Sometimes it seems the Servant is Israel; sometimes an individual who represents Israel. What is clear is that the Servant will suffer and that his sufferings will be redemptive. Jeremy Treat says: '[Isaiah] 52:13–53:12 portrays an action of salvation that is *by a servant-king* (identity) and *for a kingdom of servants* (accomplishment).'[2] Treat concludes: 'Our journey through the Old Testament revealed an unfolding pattern of royal victory through atoning sacrifice.'[3]

2.   Treat, *The Crucified King*, 85.
3.   ibid., 68.

The kingdom comes in Jesus

In Mark 1 Jesus begins his ministry by announcing the coming of God's kingdom and calling upon people to repent (1:15). Jesus is re-establishing God's rule. Matthew talks about 'the kingdom of heaven', but this is simply an accommodation to the Jewish convention of avoiding the use of God's name.

Jesus is the son of David – the promised King. He is the Messiah. The kingdom has come because the King has come. Gabriel says to Mary: 'You will be with child and give birth to a son, and you are to give him the name Jesus. He will be great and will be called the Son of the Most High. The Lord God will give him the throne of his father David, and he will reign over the house of Jacob for ever; his kingdom will never end' (Luke 1:31-33).

Jesus not only re-establishes God's rule over Israel. Israel was always intended by God to be the vehicle for the salvation of the world. And Jesus is not only the new David. He is the new Adam. He restores humanity's rule over creation under the rule of God. The antecedents for the kingdom of God that Jesus inaugurates are not simply the reign of God's king over God's people, but the reign of humanity in Adam over creation.

In 1:21-45 Mark presents a series of events that take place in a twenty-four hour period. It is as if Mark starts his portrait of Jesus with a snapshot of a typical day. The day is prefaced with Jesus calling disciples who leave all to follow him, thereby demonstrating his authority over people (1:16-20). On the Sabbath he teaches in the synagogue of Capernaum with an authority that his hearers find remarkable (1:21-28). He exorcizes a demon-possessed man. In the afternoon he heals Peter's mother-in-law who is immediately able to serve him (1:29-31). Then in the evening he heals 'all who were ill and demon-possessed' (1:32-34). Finally, in the early hours of the following morning, he heals a man with leprosy, restoring not only his physical body, but restoring him to the social body of Israel (1:40-45). A few days later he even claims authority to forgive sins (2:1-12), a claim he can substantiate with the healing of a paralysed man.

In 4:35–5:43 Mark presents an even more co-ordinated account of the authority of Jesus through four pictures that together show how comprehensive it is:

1. Authority over the natural world (4:35-41)
Jesus calms the storm with just a word and the sea is immediately still. In the Old Testament only God can control the sea (Pss. 89:8-9; 106:9). Jesus is exercising the reign of God over nature.

2. Authority over the spirit world (5:1-20)
In the next story Jesus heals a demon-possessed man. The legion of demons in the man ask Jesus if they can enter some pigs and we are told 'he gave them permission' (5:13). The demons are subject to the reign of God in Jesus.

3. Authority over sickness (5:24-34)
Mark emphasis that the next person Jesus encounters has an intractable illness that has proved beyond the scope of doctors. It is also a disease that made her perpetually unclean and so involved social ostracization. To touch this woman was yourself to become unclean. But when she touches Jesus, instead of Jesus becoming unclean, the woman becomes clean.

4. Authority over death (5:21–43)

In the final story we see the authority of Jesus even over death as he raises the daughter of Jairus from the dead. Mark presents the stories of the woman and Jairus' daughter as a 'sandwich' which the story of the woman contained within the beginning and end of the story of Jairus' daughter. Jairus' daughter is also the same age as the length of time the woman has been suffering. Mark is tying these stories together to present a complete picture of the authority of Jesus. And he presents the story of Jairus' daughter to imply that Jesus can raise someone from death as easily as we might raise someone from sleep.

In Mark 4:41 the disciples ask themselves, 'Who is this?' The answer that Mark is driving us towards is that Jesus is the King with authority over nature, spirits, sickness and even death. The kingdom has come with the coming of the King. But this is not the full picture as we will see in the next chapter.

Three

THE KING WHO COMES: THE KINGDOM COMES IN SECRET

In the previous chapter we saw that Jesus is the promised King with the authority to restore God's reign over the world. But there is a surprise. God's kingdom has come because God's King has come. But Jesus is also opposed and rejected.

THE KING IS REJECTED

Mark opens his account of the ministry of Jesus with a description of twenty-four hours in which the authority of Jesus as King is evident. But this is followed in Mark 2:1–3:6 with a sequence of stories that show the kingdom being despised, rejected and challenged. And Mark shows that opposition deepening. In the first story the criticism is unspoken (2:6). Then teachers of the law criticise

Jesus indirectly to his disciples (2:16). Subsequently they express their criticism directly to Jesus, but it is about his disciples (2:23-24). And in the final story Jesus asks them a question and they are silenced (3:4). After that the opposition widens. In 3:22 the teachers of the law come from Jerusalem; local opposition becomes national opposition. And the opposition deepens as Jesus' own family accuse him of being mad.

Mark wants us to recall Isaiah 53. Isaiah talks about a Suffering Servant – one who will come to save God's people, but will suffer. He will be despised and rejected. And that is how Mark portrays Jesus. Jesus is the Suffering Servant of Isaiah.

How can this be the coming of God's kingdom? This is not what people expected. The Jews expected the kingdom of God to come in great glory, sweeping away God's enemies and vindicating his people. So is this the real thing? Is Jesus the real thing? The evidence is mixed. In this climate of opposition and rejection, can we really say that the kingdom has come?

John the Baptist articulates this question in Matthew 11:1-6. John expected, like all good Jews, the Day of the Lord, the day of God's judgment, when everyone would acknowledge God, when the wicked would be destroyed and the righteous vindicated (Matt. 3:10). Yet John finds himself in prison and Herod still on the throne. It appears to have all gone wrong. What's going on? Is Jesus really the One who was to come or should we expect someone else?

THE SECRET OF THE KINGDOM
The kingdom is near because the King has come. But there is a credibility problem. There is a reality gap because life in

this world just goes on the same. Most people reject Jesus or just ignore him. God does not appear to be reigning in glory and triumph.

Or think about Mark's readers. They were told that Jesus has risen in triumph, ascended to the right hand of God and been given all authority. And yet life just went on the same: buying and selling, giving birth and growing old – all very ordinary. In fact it was worse than ordinary because they also faced opposition, rejection and apathy.

In response to these questions, Jesus tells a series of parables about the kingdom in Mark 4:1-34. In 4:1 we read: 'On another occasion, Jesus began to teach by the lake.' In other words chapter four is linked thematically – rather than chronologically – with what precedes it. The teaching of chapter 4 will explain the events of chapters 2-3. The stories of chapters 2-3 are stories of rejection. But if the message of Jesus is rejected, how can he be right when he proclaims the coming of God's kingdom?

The chapter consists of three parables of seeds. Though each parable brings out a different dimension of the process, each parable speaks of the present hiddenness of the kingdom – it is like a small seed – and each parable speaks of the future glory of the kingdom – the seed produces a harvest. For example:

> [Jesus] also said, 'This is what the kingdom of God is like. A man scatters seed on the ground. Night and day, whether he sleeps or gets up, the seed sprouts and grows, though he does not know how. All by itself the soil produces corn – first the stalk, then the ear, then the full grain in the ear. As soon as the grain is ripe, he puts the sickle to it, because the harvest has come.'

Again he said, 'What shall we say the kingdom of God is like, or what parable shall we use to describe it? It is like a mustard seed, which is the smallest seed you plant in the ground. Yet when planted, it grows and becomes the largest of all garden plants, with such big branches that the birds of the air can perch in its shade' (Mark 4:26-32).

A mustard seed was proverbially small. It appears insignificant. In the same way, at present, the kingdom is small and hidden. But one day it will be like the largest of trees. The kingdom has come and it is coming.

1. The kingdom has come secretly in grace
In Mark 4:11 Jesus says: 'The secret of the kingdom of God has been given to you.' The kingdom comes secretly. The Jews expected the kingdom would come in triumph. God would sweep away all his enemies in a blaze of glory and power. But the secret of the kingdom is that even though this has not happened, the kingdom has come. It has come secretly. It has come in a hidden way. The parables of this chapter illustrate this point. The kingdom of God is like a seed (4:3, 26) – indeed it is like the smallest of seeds (4:31).

2. The kingdom will come triumphantly in glory
Was the Jewish expectation therefore wrong? Did the coming of God's kingdom in secret mean it would not come in glory and power? No, the Old Testament repeatedly speaks of 'the day of the Lord' when God will be triumphant over his enemies and vindicate his people. The parables of this chapter affirm that the kingdom will come in glory. We are not to suppose that because the kingdom has come in secret and in grace that it will not

also come in glory and in judgment. The parables of this chapter speak not only of the hiddenness of the kingdom in the present, but also of the harvest it will produce in the future.

Matthew 13 contains a similar series of parables addressing the same issue.

> Jesus told them another parable: 'The kingdom of heaven is like a man who sowed good seed in his field. But while everyone was sleeping, his enemy came and sowed weeds among the wheat, and went away. When the wheat sprouted and formed ears, then the weeds also appeared. The owner's servants came to him and said, "Sir, didn't you sow good seed in your field? Where then did the weeds come from?" "An enemy did this," he replied. The servants asked him, "Do you want us to go and pull them up?" "No," he answered, "because while you are pulling the weeds, you may root up the wheat with them. Let both grow together until the harvest. At that time I will tell the harvesters: First collect the weeds and tie them in bundles to be burned; then gather the wheat and bring it into my barn."' ...
>
> Then he left the crowd and went into the house. His disciples came to him and said, 'Explain to us the parable of the weeds in the field.'
>
> He answered, 'The one who sowed the good seed is the Son of Man. The field is the world, and the good seed stands for the sons of the kingdom. The weeds are the sons of the evil one, and the enemy who sows them is the devil. The harvest is the end of the age, and the harvesters are angels. As the weeds are pulled up and burned in the fire, so it will be at the end of the age. The Son of Man will send out his angels, and they will weed out of

his kingdom everything that causes sin and all who do evil. They will throw them into the fiery furnace, where there will be weeping and gnashing of teeth. Then the righteous will shine like the sun in the kingdom of their Father. He who has ears, let him hear' (Matt. 13:24-30, 36-43).

Just because the kingdom has *not* come in glory and judgment does not mean it has not come. And just because it *has* come secretly does not mean it will not come in glory and judgment in the future. This is why Jesus speaks in parables.

The disciples came to him and asked, 'Why do you speak to the people in parables?'

He replied, 'The knowledge of the secrets of the kingdom of heaven has been given to you, but not to them. Whoever has will be given more, and he will have an abundance. Whoever does not have, even what he has will be taken from him. This is why I speak to them in parables:

"Though seeing, they do not see;

though hearing, they do not hear or understand."

In them is fulfilled the prophecy of Isaiah:

"You will be ever hearing but never understanding;

you will be ever seeing but never perceiving.

For this people's heart has become calloused;

they hardly hear with their ears,

and they have closed their eyes.

Otherwise they might see with their eyes,

hear with their ears,

understand with their hearts and turn,

and I would heal them."

But blessed are your eyes because they see, and your ears because they hear. For I tell you the truth, many prophets and righteous men longed to see what you see but did not see it, and to hear what you hear but did not hear it' (Matt. 13:10-17).

The reason Jesus speaks in parables is because the secrets of the kingdom have been given to the disciples and the secret is that, while the coming of the kingdom in glory is still in the future, the kingdom has already come in a hidden way. It has come, as it were, in advance of itself.

The parables do not contain some esoteric knowledge for insiders. These 'secrets' are not the deep truths of the kingdom which only a few can appreciate and only after years of contemplation, reflection and study. No, these secrets have been given to the disciples – hardly the world's greatest theologians or thinkers! So the parables did not contain special knowledge for the few. Rather they announce the kingdom. They declare the secret of its arrival. But they do so in such a way that those with ears to hear are enlightened while those dulled by unbelief are condemned. They further harden the hard-hearted while enlightening those with ears to hear. The parable of the sower contrasts these two responses.

In Matthew 13:14-15 Jesus quotes from Isaiah 6. The story of Isaiah's commission is familiar and verses 1-8 of Isaiah 6 are often used as a rallying cry to mission. But the verses that Jesus quotes – verses 9-10 – are used less often! Isaiah is called to a ministry that will bring judgment on the people by further and ultimately hardening their hearts. His words are not only *a message* of judgment. They are also *the means* of judgment.

Understandably Isaiah is somewhat taken aback. 'For how long, O Lord?' he asks. 'How long' must I undertake such a bitter task? The answer comes in verses 11-13 and a reference to the exile into Babylon. Isaiah must speak until Israel goes into exile. In the Bible the exile is a paradigm for the judgment of God. So it will be for those people of Jesus' day who reject him. They will experience the judgment of God just as the people of Israel did when they rejected the prophetic word. So it is for all who reject Jesus in any age.

Then in verses 16-17 Jesus turns to his disciples. Just as the hardened people of Jesus' day stand in succession with the hardened of Isaiah's day, so the disciples stand in succession with the prophets and those who did not harden their hearts. The difference is this: all that the prophets longed to see is being fulfilled in Jesus before the disciples' very eyes. That, after all, is the secret of the kingdom and that is why the disciples are so blessed.

In Mark 3:20-21 we read how Jesus is rejected by his family – they accuse him of being mad. In 3:22-30 we read how the leaders of Israel rejected Jesus – they accuse him of being in league with Satan. The location of these accusations in Mark's Gospel is significant. Mark 3:13-19 describes Jesus choosing the twelve. Mark wants us to realise that the twelve disciples are the new Israel. There are twelve disciples to match the twelve tribes of Israel. This is the new people of God. Then in 3:31-35 Jesus describes his disciples as his mother and brothers. Jesus is calling into being a new family – the new family of God. In the midst of this opposition and rejection, a new community is born. The kingdom comes to or in or through a new community, a new people, a new family.

THE SECRET OF THE KINGDOM AND THE CROSS

The secret of the kingdom lies behind the so-called 'messianic secret'. A recognition of how this works will be a first step in tying the message of the kingdom with the message of the cross.

The 'messianic secret' is the term scholars have used to describe the curious way in which Jesus repeatedly attempts to keep his identity secret in all the Synoptic Gospels, but particularly in Mark's Gospel.

> Just then a man in their synagogue who was possessed by an evil spirit cried out, 'What do you want with us, Jesus of Nazareth? Have you come to destroy us? I know who you are – the Holy One of God!' 'Be quiet!' said Jesus sternly. 'Come out of him!' (Mark 1:23-25).

> Immediately the leprosy left him and he was cured. Jesus sent him away at once with a strong warning: 'See that you don't tell this to anyone' (Mark 1:42-44).

> [Jesus] gave them strict orders not to tell who he was (Mark 3:12).

> 'But what about you?' [Jesus] asked. 'Who do you say I am?' Peter answered, 'You are the Christ.' Jesus warned them not to tell anyone about him (Mark 8:29-30).

What is the explanation for the so-called 'messianic secret'? Why should Jesus want to keep his identity quiet? Why should someone committed to preaching (1:38-39) forbid it? To understand this and see the connection to the cross we need to go to the beginning and to the centre of Mark's Gospel.

Mark begins: 'The beginning of the gospel about Jesus Christ, the Son of God' (1:1). The word 'gospel' does not refer to the literary genre (which Mark is in the process of inventing). It refers to the 'good news', the message of Jesus. And the good news involves two claims about Jesus: Jesus is the Messiah and the Son of God.

At the centre point of the Gospel is Peter's confession that Jesus is the Messiah: "'But what about you?" [Jesus] asked. "Who do you say I am?" Peter answered, "You are the Christ"' (8:29). Part one of the Gospel (Mark 1-8) is full of evidence that Jesus is the Son of God and this comes to a climax in Peter's confession.

Peter's confession follows the story of a blind man whose eyes are opened by Jesus in 8:22-26. In 8:18 the disciples have eyes but fail to see. In 8:29 Peter sees who Jesus is. In Matthew's account Jesus says, 'God has revealed this to you, Peter' (Matt. 16:17). Mark makes the same point by placing the healing of the blind man in between the unbelief and belief of the disciples. Mark wants us to realise that the disciples understand who Jesus is just as the blind man sees. Faith is God's work in us.

But we are only half way there. This feels like a climax and indeed it is. But it is only the climax of the first half of the Gospel. We have eight chapters to go. And that is because the disciples are only half way there. They see, but they do not see fully.

Jesus heals the blind man in 8:22-26 in two stages. At first the man sees only partially. 'I see people; they look like trees walking around,' he says (8:24). This healing, as we have seen, is designed to illustrate the process by which the disciples come to faith in Jesus the King. The reason the miracle is in two stages is that the disciples are only half way there. They see that Jesus is the King. Now they must see that he is the King who must suffer and die. He is the King who rules through sacrificial love.

Mark continues: 'He then began to teach them that the Son of Man must suffer ...' (8:31). The 'then' is not so much an indication of time as of their recognition. Now that they have recognised him as the messiah, Jesus can began to tell them what it really means to be the messiah of God. Now that they have learnt lesson one, he can start on lesson two. We are told, 'He spoke plainly about this ...' (8:32).

The disciples assume that messiahship means exercising power and glory. Jesus needs to re-programme their thinking. 'He spoke plainly about this, and Peter took him aside and began to rebuke him. But when Jesus turned and looked at his disciples, he rebuked Peter. "Get behind me, Satan!" he said. "You do not have in mind the things of God, but the things of men"' (Mark 8:32-33). A few minutes ago – quite literally – Peter makes a great, climactic statement of faith. Now he is doing Satan's work. It is a dramatic turnaround. But it is because he only partially sees who Jesus is. He is like the blind man at Bethsaida seeing people walking about like trees. Peter sees that Jesus is the King, but he cannot accept that Jesus is the King who must suffer and die. Recognising Jesus as the messiah is only half way to recognising the true nature of his mission and work.

The first half of Mark's Gospel climaxes in Peter's confession: Jesus is the Christ. The second half is about Jesus on the way to Jerusalem and that means on the way to the cross. The cross, the way of sacrificial love, dominates the second half of the Gospel. And this second

half climaxes in another confession, the confession of the
Centurion that Jesus is the Son of God. But this confession
is made as he sees Jesus die on the cross.

It is fallen human nature to look for God in the great
acts of creation or in great miracles. Jesus does these things:
he calms the storm, he casts out evil spirits, he heals the
sick and raises the dead. But the fullest revelation of God
is not in power and glory, but in the foolishness, ignominy
and weakness of the cross. The cross is the demonstration
of the extent of God's love. The cross is what he will do
to rescue us from our sin. The cross is how he achieves his
victory. The cross is how he exercises his reign. The One
on the throne of heaven is the Lamb who was slain. God
hides himself from the powerful and wise of this world
to ensure the graciousness of his kingdom. Only through
faith, graciously given to us by God, do we recognise in
the crucified One our Saviour and our King. The Gospels
are stories moving towards the cross and resurrection.
They have a plot which comes to a climax at the cross.

We are now in a position to understand the reason for
the 'messianic secret'. Jesus does not want his identity revealed until people realise he is the messiah who must suffer
and die. If people think of him simply as a triumphant, all-
conquering messiah they will misunderstand him. He does
not want people to follow a king of power and glory. He
wants us to follow the servant King. As we shall see, following Jesus means following him along the way of the cross.
'Then he called the crowd to him along with his disciples
and said: "If anyone would come after me, he must deny
himself and take up his cross and follow me"' (Mark 8:34).

We meet the 'messianic secret' again in 9:9-10. There is
to be no proclamation of glory until after the cross. During

the Transfiguration the voice from heaven declares: 'This is my Son, whom I love. Listen to him!' (Mark 9:7). We might expect the voice to say, 'Gaze upon him'. After all, his appearance has been transformed. But the disciples are told to 'listen' to him. Why? Because they had just refused to listen to his teaching on the cross. In 8:32 Peter rebukes Jesus for speaking plainly about the cross. As they come down from the mountain Jesus tells Peter, James and John not to tell anyone what they had seen (9:9-10). They have seen his glory, but they have not yet listened to his words about the cross.

Jesus will not let people proclaim him as King and Christ and Saviour until they have understood that he is the King who has come to serve his people, the Christ who is forsaken, the Saviour who saves by dying. There can be no proclamation of Jesus as King without the cross. Jesus forbids evangelism that focuses on healing and power and victory without the cross. Jesus does not allow any proclamation that does not focus on the cross.

The suffering of the messiah becomes the main theme of the second half of the Gospel. Mark is no longer concerned to demonstrate the authority of the king. Now his concern is to demonstrate the suffering of the king.

So there is only one miracle in the second half of the Gospel. And this exception is itself significant. Throughout Mark there is a theme of seeing (4:11-12; 8:17). Only to some is it given to see the kingdom. The disciples must have their eyes opened to recognise Jesus as the messianic King. The one miracle in the second half of the Gospel is in 10:46-52 where Jesus heals another blind man. The significant feature of this is that Jesus asks Bartimaeus: 'What do you want me to do for you?' (Mark 10:51). It is

word for word the same question he has just asked James
and John in 10:36. James and John ask for glory without
the cross. They want to bypass the cross. They want to be
aligned to a king who does not suffer. They do not 'see'
that Jesus is the King who must suffer. They need to be
given spiritual sight or insight in much the same way that
Bartimaeus needs to receive physical sight.

In history the kingdom is hidden. The world does not
recognise Jesus as Lord. His kingdom grows secretly as
his word is proclaimed. And the same pattern is seen
in his followers. We receive life through his word, but
that life is hidden. Only at the return of Christ will it
be revealed (Col. 3:1-4). In the present, our union with
Christ in his resurrection is revealed in a hidden way,
in our union with Christ in his death. It is through
resurrection power that we follow the way of the cross
(2 Cor. 4:7-18; Phil. 3:10-11).[1]

Mark's Gospel comes to a climax in 15:39: 'And when
the centurion, who stood there in front of Jesus, heard his
cry and saw how he died, he said, "Surely this man was
the Son of God!"' It is the most extraordinary statement.
What is it that the Centurion hears? He hears Jesus cry,
'My God, why have you forsaken me?' And what does
he see? He sees Jesus die in shame and weakness. And
from this he concludes, 'Surely this man was the Son of
God.' At the moment at which God is most absent, the
Centurion sees the presence of God.

Yet this is the climax of Mark's Gospel. This is where
it has all been heading. This verse pulls it all together. 1:1
provides the structure of the book. The verse makes two

---

1.   For more on this theme see Tim Chester, *The Ordinary Hero: Living the
      Cross and Resurrection*, (IVP/The Good Book Company, 2009/2013).

claims about Jesus: he is the Messiah and the Son of God. As we have seen, the confession by Peter that Jesus is the Messiah is the climax of the first part of the Gospel. Now this confession by the Centurion – a Gentile at that – is the climax of the Gospel as a whole. This final declaration ties the Gospel together.

Those who claim we do not take the Jesus of the Gospels seriously are often themselves not taking the Gospels seriously as literary unities with a distinctive message. They drop in on isolated stories to present Jesus as a model. If you view the Gospels in this selective way then it is all too easy to impose your own agenda on the text. The reality is the Gospels have a plot line and message that leads to the cross.

In 15:29-32 the Jewish leaders expect that the sign of the Christ is that he will come down from the cross. Even at the last they do not understand what sort of a Christ the Christ of God is to be. Jesus is the Christ, but for Jesus this means dying.

In 15:32 the religious leaders say: 'Let this Christ, this King of Israel, come down now from the cross, that we may see and believe.' Again we meet the theme of physical sight and spiritual insight. They want to see something that will make them believe. But they are blind. They think the Christ will be revealed if he comes down from the cross. But it is by staying *on* the cross that Jesus reveals God. It is as the Centurion *'saw how he died'* that he recognises in Jesus the Son of God.

If the death of Jesus redefines the nature of kingship, the resurrection of Jesus confirms that the crucified One is God's promised King. God has made Jesus Lord and

King by raising him from the dead. This was the message
of the apostles. They saw the Old Testament promise of a
coming King fulfilled in the resurrection.

> 'God has raised this Jesus to life, and we are all witnesses
> of the fact … Therefore let all Israel be assured of this:
> God has made this Jesus, whom you crucified, both Lord
> and Christ' (Acts 2:32, 36).

> 'We tell you the good news: What God promised our
> fathers he has fulfilled for us, their children, by raising up
> Jesus. As it is written in the second Psalm: "You are my
> Son; today I have become your Father"' (Acts 13:32-33).

A GLIMPSE OF THE COMING KINGDOM

The two comings of the kingdom are not two separate
realities. There is only one kingdom. The miracles of Jesus
are a glimpse of the coming kingdom. They are a pointer
and promise of what is to come. The salvation that Jesus
offers is not simply an abstract or ethereal salvation. It is
not the salvation of Gnosticism which offered knowledge
that would enable you to transcend the physical world.
Jesus promises the *restoration* of the physical world.

Consider, for example, how Luke handles the same
four stories that Mark presents to show the authority of
Jesus over the natural world, the spirit world, sickness and
death (Mark 4:35-5:43). Luke presents these stories in
Luke 8 and sets them up as signs of the new world that
Jesus will create through his death and resurrection.

In Luke 8:48 Jesus says, 'Daughter, your faith has
healed you.' But the word is actually 'saved'. 'Your faith has
saved you.' In 8:50 Jesus says, 'Don't be afraid; just believe,
and she will be healed.' Again the word is actually 'saved'.
She will be saved. Luke is a doctor. He knows plenty of

other words that he could have used to describe people getting well. But he uses the word 'salvation'. He wants us to see in these stories a sign of the salvation Jesus offers.

Our world is a world of hunger, pain and suffering. Even in the West where most people have enough to eat, we still live in want, we are still unsatisfied. We may not long for bread, but we long for meaning, intimacy, fulfilment, community, purpose and joy. We long for the world to be sorted out.

Jesus does not fit in our broken world. He bursts our expectations. His miracles are extraordinary. But this is not because what he did could not happen or did not happen. To judge his miracles by our experience is to miss the point. They do not belong in this world because they are a glimpse of another world. They are a sign of God's coming world.

The world we have created is a world of famine, injustice, division and hurt. But the kingdom of Jesus is very different. For a moment in history we were given a glimpse of that coming reality: the poor are fed; the sick are healed; the dead are raised; evil is defeated. This is the future of the kingdom of God.

In Revelation 5, John sees a vision of a scroll. The scroll represents the acts of history. Whoever is worthy to open the scroll is the one who controls history. Is there such a person? John fears not. But 'then one of the elders said to me, "Do not weep! See, the Lion of the tribe of Judah, the Root of David, has triumphed. He is able to open the scroll and its seven seals"' (Rev. 5:5). Yet when John sees the Davidic king he sees 'a Lamb, looking as if it had been slain' (Rev. 5:6). The elders and the living creatures sing: 'You are worthy to take the scroll and to open its seals, because you were slain, and with your blood you purchased men for God from every tribe and language and people and nation' (Rev. 5:9). The crucified King has triumphed. When the seventh angel sounds his trumpet, loud voices in heaven say: 'The kingdom of the world has become the kingdom of our Lord and of his Christ, and he will reign for ever and ever' (Rev. 11:15). In Revelation 21–22 we get a picture of life under the restored rule of God. It is life without threat, sin, pain, suffering or death. It is a life of blessing, abundance and security. It is a life of true freedom. The power of sin and death has been broken. We are free to be what we were intended to be – people who know and worship God. And that is good news.

Four

THE KING WHO DIES: THE KINGDOM COMES IN GRACE

We have seen that the secret of the kingdom is that it has come in the ministry of Jesus even though its full coming in glory is still in the future. The kingdom has come and is coming.

We have seen, too, that the secret of the kingdom is tied to the identity of Jesus. We cannot understand the kingship of Jesus unless we understand that he is the King who dies. Kingdom and cross are bound together to the extent that you cannot proclaim one without the other. But we still need to understand the nature of that connection.

THE GOOD NEWS AND BAD NEWS
OF THE KINGDOM OF GOD

At first sight the coming of God's kingdom is good news. Matthew makes this explicit with his phrase 'the gospel of the kingdom of heaven'. Mark makes this clear in his description of the beginning of the ministry of Jesus: 'After John was put in prison, Jesus went into Galilee, proclaiming the good news of God. "The time has come," he said. "The kingdom of God is near"' (Mark 1:14-15). Jesus proclaims good news and that good news is that 'the kingdom of God is near'.

And why would the kingdom of God not be good news? In Genesis 1 we saw that God's kingdom is a kingdom of provision and protection. Paul describes it as 'righteousness, peace and joy in the Holy Spirit' (Rom. 14:17).

'Gospel' was a word with a wider currency beyond the Christian church. In first-century Rome proclaiming 'gospel' meant proclaiming the good news that the Emperor had triumphed in battle. The herald might run ahead of the army and arrive in Rome proclaiming the 'gospel' of victory. That meant, too, that the King was coming.

In the same way the Christian gospel is the good news that Jesus has triumphed in battle. Sin and death have been defeated, and the King is coming. When he comes he will consummate the kingdom and reign without opposition. The kingdom we saw glimpsed in his miracles will be realised in full. 'He will wipe every tear from their eyes. There will be no more death or mourning or crying or pain, for the old order of things has passed away' (Rev. 21:4).

The problem is – and this is central to understanding the connection between the cross and the kingdom – the coming of God's kingdom in glory will not be good news to rebels. To those living in rebellion against God's rule the coming of his kingdom will mean defeat and disaster. And all humanity is in rebellion against God. So for us the coming of God's kingdom will mean judgment.

A number of passages connect the coming of God's kingdom with the coming of God's wrath:

- 'As surely as I live,' declares the Sovereign LORD, 'I will rule over you with a mighty hand and an outstretched arm and with outpoured wrath' (Ezek. 20:33).

- For the sins of their mouths, for the words of their lips, let them be caught in their pride. For the curses and lies they utter, consume them in wrath, consume them till they are no more. Then it will be known to the ends of the earth that God rules over Jacob (Ps. 59:12-13).

- But the LORD is the true God; he is the living God, the eternal King. When he is angry, the earth trembles; the nations cannot endure his wrath (Jer. 10:10).

The Jews longed for the coming of God's kingdom and the day of the LORD. They assumed it would mean the defeat of God's enemies. The problem was that, as the prophets warned, they were themselves God's enemies. Consider for example, Amos 5:18-20:

Woe to you who long
    for the day of the LORD!
Why do you long for the day of the LORD?
    That day will be darkness, not light.
It will be as though a man fled from a lion
    only to meet a bear,

as though he entered his house
    and rested his hand on the wall
    only to have a snake bite him.
Will not the day of the LORD be darkness, not light –
    pitch-dark, without a ray of brightness?

The people long for the day of the LORD, but it will not be the day of light they expect. It will be, even for them, a day of darkness. They think their plight at the hand of their enemies is bad. They long for God's coming because he will judge their enemies. But when God comes they will find themselves facing a far worse enemy: God himself. We find the same message in Malachi:

You have wearied the LORD with your words.
    'How have we wearied him?' you ask.
By saying, 'All who do evil are good in the eyes
    of the LORD,
    and he is pleased with them' or 'Where is
    the God of justice?'
'See, I will send my messenger, who will prepare
    the way before me.
Then suddenly the Lord you are seeking will come
    to his temple;
    the messenger of the covenant, whom you desire,
    will come,' says the LORD Almighty.
But who can endure the day of his coming?
Who can stand when he appears?
For he will be like a refiner's fire or a launderer's soap
(Mal. 2:17–3:2).

The people long for God to intervene to bring justice. They accuse God of being indifferent to evil, even favouring it, because he has not acted to defend them from their enemies. Malachi affirms that God is coming. His messenger will prepare the way for him. But, he warns, who can endure his coming? The people should not so eagerly long for God's intervention because he will come like a refiner's fire and a launderer's soap. He will establish justice, but that is not good news for all who contribute to injustice. He will refine the world of evil, but that is not good news for all those who are evil. He will cleanse the world of sin, but that is not good news for all those who are unclean.

The Malachi passage is particularly significant because it is quoted by Mark at the beginning of his Gospel. Mark parcels it up with another quote from Isaiah 40 (and follows the convention of prefacing this with a reference only to the major prophet):

> The beginning of the gospel about Jesus Christ,
> the Son of God. It is written in Isaiah the prophet:
>> 'I will send my messenger ahead of you,
>>   who will prepare your way' –
>> 'a voice of one calling in the desert,
>> "Prepare the way for the Lord,
>>   make straight paths for him"'
> (Mark 1:1-3).

Isaiah 40:3 speaks of one who will prepare for the coming of the LORD as he comes in salvation. God's coming will mean comfort for God's people (40:1) and the proclamation of the good news (40:9). Malachi 3 also refers to one who prepares for the coming of the LORD. But this time the LORD's coming will involve judgment. This one who prepares the way is, says Mark, John the Baptist (Mark 1:4). And so the One for whom he prepares is

Jesus. Jesus is the Lord coming in salvation (as promised in Isaiah) and judgment (as promised in Malachi). Mark's quotes set the agenda for his Gospel. We are to expect salvation and judgment in and through the ministry of Jesus.

JUDGMENT AND THE COMING OF GOD'S KINGDOM

It is not hard to see salvation in the ministry of Jesus. He heals the sick, releases those bound by evil spirits, feeds the hungry, raises the dead and forgives sin. But where is judgment?

In Mark 11-13 Jesus comes to the temple in Jerusalem. 'Then suddenly the Lord you are seeking will come to his temple,' says Malachi. 'But who can endure the day of his coming?' (Mal. 3:1-2). Jesus is the Lord coming to the temple in judgment and he comes to cleanse the temple which is what he does in Mark 11:1-11, 15-18. His judgment of the temple is pictured in the cursing of the fig tree (11:12-21). Jesus tells his disciples that they will replace the temple as the place of prayer and forgiveness (11:22-25). Then in chapter 12, Mark presents a series of confrontations between Jesus and the religious establishment (11:27–12:44). Finally in Mark 13, Jesus announces the destruction of the temple: 'Not one stone here will be left on another; every one will be thrown down' (13:2). But still judgment does not fall.

We find the same 'problem' in the quotes that Jesus makes from Isaiah 61. In Luke's Gospel, Jesus initiates his ministry with a quotation from Isaiah 61 in the synagogue in Nazareth before declaring that it is fulfilled. Here is the quote from Isaiah 61:1-2:

The Spirit of the Sovereign LORD is on me,
because the LORD has anointed me
to proclaim good news to the poor.
He has sent me to bind up the broken-hearted,
to proclaim freedom for the captives
and release from darkness for the prisoners,
to proclaim the year of the LORD's favour
and the day of vengeance of our God ...

And here is the quote from Luke 4:18-19:

'The Spirit of the Lord is on me,
because he has anointed me
to preach good news to the poor.
He has sent me to proclaim freedom for the prisoners
and recovery of sight for the blind,
to release the oppressed,
to proclaim the year of the Lord's favour.'

What is striking is the way Jesus omits the final line. He is about to proclaim good news, open blind eyes and release. But, it seems, he is not about to usher in the day of God's vengeance.

As we have seen, John the Baptist questions whether Jesus really is the king who will establish God's kingdom (Matt. 11:2-3). John himself announced that 'the axe is already at the root of the trees, and every tree that does not produce good fruit will be cut down and thrown into the fire' (Matt. 3:10). In other words, judgment was imminent. But the axe has not fallen. Instead, John finds himself in prison. Jesus replies with an allusion to Isaiah 35:4-6 and Isaiah 61:1-2. He is the One who fulfils the messianic expectation, the One who is bringing in God's kingdom.

But again he has edited his sources. Both passages in Isaiah refer to judgment, but Jesus omits this reference.

THE CROSS AND THE GOOD NEWS OF GOD'S KINGDOM

Jesus has come and he is bringing in God's kingdom. But judgment does not fall. Except that judgment does fall. It falls at the cross. This is the crucial point and the crucial moment in the story. This is the great surprise. This is the wonderful twist. Judgment falls not on the King's enemies, but on the King himself.

The coming of God's kingdom is good news except to those who are rebels. For rebels it means judgment and we are all rebels. The good news is that the King has borne our judgment in our place. If we return to Mark's Gospel, for example, we read:

> At the sixth hour darkness came over the whole land until the ninth hour. And at the ninth hour Jesus cried out in a loud voice, 'Eloi, Eloi, lama sabachthani?' - which means, 'My God, my God, why have you forsaken me?'
> When some of those standing near heard this, they said, 'Listen, he's calling Elijah.'
> Someone ran, filled a sponge with wine vinegar, put it on a stick, and offered it to Jesus to drink. 'Now leave him alone. Let's see if Elijah comes to take him down,' he said.
> With a loud cry, Jesus breathed his last.
> The curtain of the temple was torn in two from top to bottom (Mark 15:33-38).

Darkness is a sign in the Bible of judgment. One of the plagues on Egypt at the time of the exodus was darkness (Ps. 105:26-28). So the darkness indicates that God is judging. But who is he judging? The next verse answers this question as Jesus cries out: 'My God, my God, why have you forsaken me?' God the Father forsakes Jesus. Jesus bears the judgment we deserve. He absorbs the holy wrath of God. 'The wrath-bearing nature of Jesus' death is essential for the coming of the kingdom.'[1]

As a result the curtain of the temple is torn in two. The temple was a great lesson in the inaccessibility of God. Its purpose was to demonstrate that God was so holy and so glorious that we could not come to him. There was a court of women and Gentiles beyond which they could not go. Then a court beyond which the men could not go. Then an area in which only the priests were allowed. Beyond that, behind a great curtain, was the Holy of Holies – the ultimate symbol of God's presence. Only the High Priest could enter the Holy of Holies, and he could do so only once a year and only through the shedding of sacrificial blood (Heb. 9:7). Even then he entered with terror, for God is holy and glorious.

But as Christ makes his last cry, the curtain is torn from top to bottom. It was a thick curtain – too thick to tear by hand. And it is torn from the top. Both symbolically and literally, this is an act of God. The God who is inaccessible is suddenly accessible. God who is a consuming fire now welcomes us. The way to God is open. According to the writer to the Hebrews the temple was only a shadow of the real thing (Heb. 9:1-10). Jesus entered 'the greater and more perfect tabernacle' (Heb. 9:11). He did not enter something that symbolized the presence of God – he entered the very presence of God. He did not enter

---

1. Treat, *The Crucified King*, 132.

through the blood of sacrificed animals – he entered
through his own blood shed on the cross.

There is a terrible ironic clue to what is going on in
the mockery of Mark 15:31: 'In the same way the chief
priests and the teachers of the law mocked him among
themselves. "He saved others," they said, "but he can't
save himself!"' What they did not realise was that Jesus
does indeed save others, but he does so by refusing to save
himself. His death is our life. His forsakenness by God
makes possible our acceptance by God. His destruction is
our salvation. Donald Macleod says:

> The underlying theological fact is that the dying of
> Christ is a kingly act, not merely in the sense that he
> dies royally and with dignity, but in the sense that his
> dying is his supreme achievement for his people: the act
> by which he conquers their foes, secures their liberty and
> establishes his kingdom.[2]

As a result of the cross, the coming of God's kingdom
can be experienced as good news by all who turn to the
King in faith and repentance. Here we circle back to the
beginning of Mark's Gospel. Jesus begins his ministry
with the words: 'The time has come. The kingdom of God
is near. Repent and believe the good news!' (Mark 1:15).
The coming of the kingdom is good news to those who
repent and believe.

Forgiveness of sin is central to the coming of the
kingdom of God as good news for repentant sinners.
Treat says: 'At the forefront of Isaiah's vision for a new

exodus culminating in God's reign over the earth is the forgiveness of sins (Isa. 40:2; 43:25; 44:22; cf. 33:24), echoing the great revelation of the royal redeeming God who is "merciful and gracious … forgiving iniquity and transgression and sin" (Exod. 34:6-7).'[3] Moreover 'the forgiveness of sins was not an isolated aspect of the kingdom of God but deeply intertwined with the rest. Isaiah 40:1-2 and Zechariah 13:1-2 both place the forgiveness of sins and the defeat of evil side by side, being brought about respectively by "him whom they have pierced" (Zech. 12:10) and by him who was "pierced for our transgressions" (Isa. 53:5).'[4]

Or think of it like this. Sometimes wars come to an end because they reach a point of stalemate and both parties realise a negotiated settlement is the only way forward. But normally wars end when the strongest party wins. War is then followed by peace – or at least the cessation of conflict. In this situation the price of peace is paid by the weakest party.

God and humanity are at war. But God offers us peace. But what is the price of our surrender? Do we have the resources to pay reparations? The amazing thing about God's peace terms is that he pays the price of surrender. He pays reparations. The price of peace is borne by the Conqueror. Jesus the conquering King is defeated at the cross on our behalf. Before he comes to strike down his enemies, he is struck down.

This biblical perspective mirrors an important discussion in theology concerning whether the death of Christ

---

3.   Treat, *The Crucified King*, 133.

4.   ibid., 133.

should be seen as his victory over Satan (a view known as Christus Victor) or an act of substitution in which Jesus bears the penalty of sin that his people deserve (penal substitution). These views, however, are not alternatives or simply differing perspectives. Rather, Christ achieves his victory over Satan through his substitution because this disarms Satan's power to accuse.[5] Jeremy Treat concludes: 'Rejecting "Christus Victor versus penal substitution" and not settling for "Christus Victor and penal substitution," I propose "Christus Victor through penal substitution" … Humans are in bondage to Satan because they have rejected God as king; they are in the kingdom of Satan because they have been banished from the kingdom of God.'[6] In contrast to 'Satan the accuser,' Treat points us to 'Jesus the propitiator'.[7]

Think back to the secular usage of the term 'gospel' which was the announcement of victory in battle. Our gospel is no different. We, too, announce the victory of our King over the enemies of sin and death. But what makes our gospel glorious and gracious is that this victory is achieved through his defeat.

I recently read a book on the kingdom of God by a well-known evangelical figure. It mentions the cross just twice with half a dozen other references to the death of Jesus. All of them were passing references. My point is not that every Christian book has to talk about the cross at length. But a book on the kingdom of God must do so if it is to accurately present 'the good news of the kingdom'.

5. See Tim Chester, *Delighting in the Trinity: Why Father, Son and Spirit are Good News*, 2nd ed., (The Good Bood Company, 2010), 137-155.

6. Treat, *The Crucified King*, 199.

7. ibid., 211.

A MOMENT FOR REPENTANCE

In the previous chapter we saw that the kingdom comes secretly. It will come in great glory and triumph, but first it comes in a hidden way in the ministry of Jesus. Now we see that the kingdom comes in grace. The reason for the two-stage coming of the kingdom is to create the opportunity for faith and repentance.

This is why the ascension is so important. Jesus reigns in heaven. His reign is real. We're not engaged in an act of make-believe. We're not pretending when we say Jesus is Lord. In heaven, he has all authority. There's no doubt about his kingship.

But he has not yet come to impose his reign on earth. For that would be judgment on all those who reject him. Instead he first sends his disciples to proclaim his kingship, to call on people to repent, to call on people to find refuge in him.

Peter addresses the question of why Christ has not yet come in glory. He says: 'The Lord is not slow in keeping his promise, as some understand slowness. He is patient with you, not wanting anyone to perish, but everyone to come to repentance' (2 Pet. 3:9). The reason the kingdom of Christ has not yet come in glory and the world has not yet been sorted out and justice is not yet established on earth is that God is patient. He is waiting for his people to repent. This is how C. S. Lewis puts it:

> Another possible objection is this. Why is God landing in this enemy-occupied world in disguise and starting a sort of secret society to undermine the devil? Why is He not landing in force, invading it? Is it that He is not strong enough? Well, Christians think He is going to

land in force; we do not know when. But we can guess why He is delaying. He wants to give us the chance of joining his side freely. I do not suppose you and I would have thought much of a Frenchman who waited till the Allies were marching into Germany and then announced he was on our side. God will invade. But I wonder whether people who ask God to interfere openly and directly in our world quite realise what it will be like when He does. When that happens, it is the end of the world. When the author walks on to the stage the play is over. God is going to invade, all right: but what is the good of saying you are on his side then, when you see the whole natural universe melting away like a dream and something else – something it never entered your head to conceive – comes crashing in; something so beautiful to some of us and so terrible to others that none of us will have any choice left? For this time it will be God without disguise; something so overwhelming that it will strike either irresistible love or irresistible horror into every creature. It will be too late then to choose your side. There is no use saying you choose to lie down when it has become impossible to stand up. That will not be the time for choosing: it will be the time when we discover which side we really have chosen, whether we realised it before or not. Now, today, this moment, is our chance to choose the right side. God is holding back to give us that chance. It will not last for ever. We must take it or leave it.[8]

The chaos and pain of this world – which seep into our own lives – are a sign of God's patience. God is waiting. And that delay creates a space for mercy and for mission. God

8.   C. S. Lewis, *Mere Christianity* (1952) in C. S. Lewis, *Selected Books*, (London: HarperCollins, 1999), 360-361.

is giving people a moment to repent. God is giving us a moment to call people to repentance. But that moment will not last for ever. One day Christ will return. There is a tension here which we experience, often with tears. We long for Christ to return to end injustice. We long for Christ to delay until our loved ones have repented.

Two gospels or one

We can now evaluate our 'two gospels' and we discover they are not really two gospels, but one. The kingdom of God is the good news that God has intervened into history to restore his reign through the ministry of Jesus. That ministry was the pointer to, and promise of, the day when God will again intervene in history to consummate his kingdom to his eternal glory. This is good news because his reign is good news. It is a reign of justice, peace and joy. It is life-giving and liberating. It is a reign that encompasses not just personal forgiveness of sin, but also the restoration of all things.

But, without the message of the cross, the kingdom of God is not good news for humanity because we are all rebels and rebels will experience God's coming reign as judgment. The good news of the cross is that the King has died in our place, bearing our punishment. Through repentance and faith in the finished work of Christ we can be justified and so experience his coming reign as justice, joy and peace.

Moreover, the New Testament affirms that what has happened in our personal salvation is the beginning of the restoration of all things. James 1:18 says: 'He chose to give us birth through the word of truth, that we might be a kind of firstfruits of all he created.' In Romans 8:20-21, Paul says: 'For the creation was subjected to frustration, not by its own choice, but by the will of the one who subjected it, in hope that the creation itself will be liberated from its bondage to decay and brought into the glorious freedom of the children of God.' The freedom we already enjoy as children of God is the freedom that creation will one day enjoy. Even for us this experience is partial for we too await the redemption of our bodies. But in the meantime we have the 'firstfruits of the Spirit' (Rom. 8:23).

Titus 3:5-6 says: '[God] saved us through the washing of rebirth and renewal by the Holy Spirit, whom he poured out on us generously through Jesus Christ our Saviour.' The word Paul uses when he talks about 'the washing of rebirth' literally means 'new beginning'. The only other time it is used in the New Testament is Matthew 19:28 when Jesus says: 'I tell you the truth, at the renewal of all things, when the Son of Man sits on his glorious throne, you who have followed me will also sit on twelve thrones, judging the twelve tribes of Israel.' Jesus is not talking about a person becoming a Christian. He is talking about the renewal or the rebirth or the new beginning of all things. He is not talking about the renewal of one life, but the renewal of all life. So our rebirth and renewal by the Holy Spirit is the beginning of the rebirth and renewal of all things! What God is doing in our hearts is a glimpse of the new creation. God's new world – so radically different from our own world – has begun in your life and in the life of your church.

Five

THE KING WHO SPEAKS: THE KINGDOM COMES THROUGH THE WORD

The Bible story begins with an affirmation of the kingship of God over creation, as we have seen. But the Genesis account not only demonstrates that God reigns, but also how God reigns. 'And God said, "Let there be light," and there was light' (Gen. 1:3). He speaks and the universe comes into being (John 1:1-3). God rules through his word.

God places humanity as his vice-regents, ruling over creation under his rule. Again, God rules through his word. Adam and Eve are to express their commitment to God's rule through trust in his word.

In Genesis 3, humanity rejects God's rule. But this happens because the Serpent encourages the woman to doubt God's word (3:1) and then deny God's word (3:4).

Instead of trusting the word of God, the woman is governed by what seems 'pleasing to the eyes' (3:6). It was not that the fruit of the tree of the knowledge of good and evil was in some way intrinsically poisonous. Instead the act of eating in defiance of God's rule enacted a choice by humanity to determine for ourselves what is good and evil. God rules as his word is trusted and obeyed. God is rejected when his word is not trusted and not obeyed.

As human beings we were made to live under God's word and understand life through God's word. When we rejected that word we did not stop being interpreters. But now we look for other interpretations. People are still trying to understand life through words. We tell stories and create ideologies to make sense of our lives. God's revelation is all around us (Rom. 1:19-20), so some aspects of these interpretations align with God's word. But we suppress the truth in our wickedness (Rom. 1:18). We fill our lives with self-justifying stories. 'They exchanged the truth of God for a lie, and worshipped and served created things rather than the Creator – who is for ever praised. Amen' (Rom. 1:25).

The story of salvation is the story of God re-establishing his rule. It begins with the promise to Abraham. And it is important to recognise that a promise is a word about the future. God rules through his word and he begins the process of re-establishing his rule through his word (in the form of a promise).

We see the same pattern when God liberates Israel from Egypt. He leads them to Mount Sinai where he gives them a word (in the form of a law). The promise to Abraham is re-stated in the covenant made through

Moses. This law is to govern the life of God's redeemed people. The law of Sinai was not given as a means of salvation. It points forward to the gospel of Jesus Christ. The law of Moses was the word by which God ruled his people as they waited for the coming Saviour. The law of Moses was not Plan A that went wrong so forcing God to come up with Plan B in Jesus. The law finds its fulfilment in the gospel. Law and gospel only become opposites when people see the law as the means of salvation. It is salvation by works and salvation by faith which are the true opposites.

Samuel is described as a judge. But when he anoints Saul as king, he begins to be known as a prophet. There had been prophets before – Moses and Deborah are described as prophets. But the prophet as an institution arises with the monarchy. The king is to rule under God's rule expressed through his word. That is what God said in Deuteronomy 17 when he anticipated the people's request for a king. The prophets proclaim this word. The prophet guides the king so that the king rules under God's authority. That was the ideal. More often, however, the prophet had to call the king back to God's word.

Often the word of the prophet and the rule of the king are in conflict. We see this conflict in the reign of the first king, Saul. Saul gets off to a good start, but soon his reign unravels. Saul is told to destroy the Amalekites and all their possessions, but he saves the best of their sheep and oxen for sacrifice. Samuel says that God has rejected Saul as king because what counts is not sacrifice, but obedience to God's word. God rejects Saul when Saul rejects God's reign expressed through God's word (1 Sam. 15:22-23). In contrast to those kings who challenged or avoided God's

word (2 Kings 1:1-17), those who rule in obedience to
God's word are commended (2 Kings 18:3-6).

When the word of God comes into conflict with the
king it is God's word that wins. The pattern is set by
Jeroboam, the first king of the ten northern tribes after
they have broken away from the Davidic kingdom.

> By the word of the LORD a man of God came from Judah
> to Bethel, as Jeroboam was standing by the altar to make
> an offering. He cried out against the altar by the word
> of the LORD: 'O altar, altar! This is what the LORD says:
> "A son named Josiah will be born to the house of David.
> On you he will sacrifice the priests of the high places
> who now make offerings here, and human bones will be
> burned on you."' That same day the man of God gave a
> sign: 'This is the sign the LORD has declared: The altar
> will be split apart and the ashes on it will be poured out.'
>
> When King Jeroboam heard what the man of God
> cried out against the altar at Bethel, he stretched out his
> hand from the altar and said, 'Seize him!' But the hand
> he stretched out towards the man shrivelled up, so that
> he could not pull it back. Also, the altar was split apart
> and its ashes poured out according to the sign given by
> the man of God by the word of the LORD. Then the king
> said to the man of God, 'Intercede with the LORD your
> God and pray for me that my hand may be restored.'
> So the man of God interceded with the LORD, and the
> king's hand was restored and became as it was before
> (1 Kings 13:1-6).

This is part of a section that begins 'by the word of the Lord'
and ends: 'the word of the LORD ... will certainly come
true' (1 Kings 13:32). An unnamed man of God comes
to Jeroboam to predict the downfall of the golden calves

Jeroboam has erected. Jeroboam tries to stop the prophet as if by so doing he could stop God's word operating. He pits his authority against the authority of God's word. He tries to turn back God's word like King Canute trying to turn back the tide. It cannot be done and his outstretched hand shrivels up. God does his work through his word. God's word drives the story. It determines events. It not only informs, warns and predicts. It actually causes things to happen.

This is followed by a strange story (1 Kings 13:7-32) in which the man of God is deceived into disobeying God's word. What is clear is that the prophet tragically becomes an illustration of his own message. God's word is certain. Even though the man of God from Judah cannot be held culpable because he was tricked, he still dies in fulfilment of God's word (1 Kings 13:26). How much more certain is God's word of judgment against Jeroboam (1 Kings 13:32).

This pattern of conflict between the king and the prophet is repeated throughout the stories of Israel's kings with the word of God continually proving to be sovereign. In 1 Kings 22:1-28 Ahab's prophets know what he wants to hear and that is what they tell him. He chooses their counsel and does not seek that of the prophet Micaiah because he does not like what Micaiah says (22:8). Ahab chooses to hear what he wants to hear. But Micaiah demonstrates how foolish that is. The messenger advises him to tell Ahab what Ahab wants to hear (22:13). Micaiah replies by saying that a prophet can only speak from God. He cannot give his own message or a message to order. He can no more make up a message from God than the messenger can make up a message from the king.

Imagine if the messenger ignored what the king told him and made something else up instead. He would not last long in the king's service. What is the point of a prophet who does not speak from God? At first reading, Micaiah goes back in verse 15 on what he has said in verse 14. In reality it is the same message, but delivered with greater force through the use of irony. In other words, in verse 15 Micaiah says what the king wants to hear, but with such a lack of conviction that it is obvious to everyone that what he says is worthless.

In 1 and 2 Kings the warnings of Deuteronomy slowly unfold as the nation turns from God. The book of Deuteronomy promised blessings if the people were obedient, but it also outlined curses if they were not faithful to the covenant (Deut. 28 and 30). This is the principle by which the writer of Kings interprets history. What happens to Israel, happens because those curses come into play. God's word is sovereign and so there is something inexorable about the story. The disaster that falls on Israel is a result of the judging and destroying power of God's law. God's word sets in train events which cannot be altered.

As we have seen, through the ministry of Jesus the kingdom has come in a secret and gracious way. But it is also true that God continues to rule through his word and he extends his rule through his word. The kingdom grows as 'the message of the kingdom' (Matt. 13:19) is proclaimed and when a person 'hears the word and understands it' (Matt. 13:23).

In Luke's Gospel, Jesus proclaims his 'manifesto' in Luke 4:18-19: 'The Spirit of the Lord is on me, because he has anointed me to preach good news to the poor. He has sent me to proclaim freedom for the prisoners and recovery of sight for the blind, to release the oppressed, to proclaim the year of the Lord's favour.' Jesus says that he is the One who will fulfil God's promise of a new world. That is a big claim and in Luke 4:31-44 Luke demonstrates that Jesus can deliver. He describes the events in one twenty-four hour period to show the power of Jesus. There are three scenes in which we see:

1. The power of Jesus over an evil spirit (vv. 31-37).

2. The power of Jesus over illness (vv. 38-39).

3. The power of Jesus over every demon and every illness (vv. 40-41).

In each case, Jesus restores completely and immediately. In the first episode, Jesus simply speaks and the demon must leave. The possessed man is left uninjured (v. 35). It is complete liberation with no side-effects and people are amazed (v. 36). With Peter's mother-in-law, Luke the doctor adds (uniquely in the Gospels) that this was a 'high' fever. But again Jesus speaks and the fever leaves. Moreover, there is no need for convalescence. 'At once' she is able to serve others (v. 39). As a result, news quickly gets around and many come for healing or for exorcism. Luke says 'all' who had 'various kinds' of illness come to him and Jesus healed 'each one'. Jesus has power over every illness and every evil. He has the power to deliver God's new world.

But Luke also highlights the means by which Jesus rules. 'Jesus said sternly' in verse 35 is literally 'rebuked'. The same word is used in verses 39 and 41: Jesus rebukes the evil spirit and the illness (vv. 35, 39). All three episodes contain the same word, 'rebuke'.

A rebuke is an exercise of authority. You can rebuke
me if I am your employee or your child or a member of
your church. But not if I am a stranger. Then you would be
a mad man ranting in the street! A rebuke is an exercise
of authority. So these miracles show who Jesus is: God's
promised Saviour-King. But these stories also show that
Jesus establishes his kingdom through his word. Jesus casts out
evil spirits and heals the sick with just a word.

Verse 32 says: 'They were amazed at his teaching, because his words had authority.' What was it about Jesus
that amazed the people who saw him? His love? His miracles? His antagonism to the religious leaders? Perhaps.
But it was certainly the authority of his word. That is what
Luke highlights. Again, verse 36 says: 'All the people were
amazed and said to each other, "What words these are!
With authority and power he gives orders to impure spirits and they come out!"' There is authority and power in
the word of Jesus.

God works through his word. God created the universe
through his word. God initiated the plan of salvation in
Abraham through his word. God gathered his people at
Sinai through his word. God ruled the history of Israel
through the word of his prophets. God promised to
raise God's people from the dry bones through his word
(Ezek. 37). And now God's king has come and he rules
through his word. He extends his reign through his word.
In verse 34 the evil spirit tries to disrupt the teaching of
Jesus. If we doubt God's word or if we neglect God's word
or if we cast doubt on God's word, then we are doing
Satan's work.

God's word must be central to our lives, our churches
and our mission. Picture what would happen if these

miracles took place in your neighbourhood. Huge crowds would gather. Hospital wards would empty. Jesus appears to have made it. He is big news. He is attracting big crowds. But he turns his back on it all. Why? 'I must proclaim the good news of the kingdom of God to the other towns also, because that is why I was sent' (v. 43). The miracles are a distraction. The people try to keep him from leaving (v. 42). But his priority is different from their priorities. His priority is proclamation. Why?

1. The cross at the centre of our message

The miracles are signs to God's coming world. But they are only signs. What matters is God's coming kingdom. 'I must proclaim the good news of the kingdom of God' (Luke 4:43). Jesus does not want people to get caught up with the sign and miss where it is pointing.

Imagine a child entranced by a brightly coloured sign to Disneyland and refusing to leave it. 'It's so lovely,' she might say. 'But the real thing is just down the road!' That is what the crowds are like. 'Do some more miracles,' they demand. 'But the real thing is down the road,' says Jesus. If you mistake the sign for the reality then you will never take up your cross and follow Jesus (Luke 9:23-26). If your focus is on present miracles, present blessing, present prosperity, then you will never deny yourself or lose your life for Jesus. And so you will not gain your life when Jesus returns.

The priority of Jesus is proclamation because the focus of his ministry is the cross. The great saving event in the ministry of Jesus is not the exorcism of the man in the temple nor the healing of Peter's mother-in-law. It is the cross. The miracles save people temporarily. But they are only a sign. It is the cross which saves completely.

Demonic possession and sickness are a result of humanity's rebellion against God. Our sin has fractured creation and we are now under the curse of God. Jesus reverses the effects of the curse as a sign of his work. But his real work is to address the underlying causes – the problem of sin and judgment. And that is what he will do at the cross when he takes our sin and endures our punishment in our place.

It is sometimes pointed out that the preaching of the gospel in the book of Acts includes rather few references to the cross. From this it is inferred that the cross is not central to apostolic preaching. At one level this is hard to deny and there is an important lesson for us. But that lesson is not that the cross is peripheral to the apostolic gospel.

Every sermon in Acts is different because each was addressed to a different situation. But there is a common pattern:

a.   Christ has died.

b.   Christ has risen.

c.   The apostles are witnesses to this.

d.   God now offers forgiveness.

The event of the cross is central and the fruit of the cross is central. What is not central is the mechanism which connects the event and its fruit. That is important, which is why it features in the letters to the apostolic churches. Christians need to know about the atonement and penal substitution because it safeguards the grace of God and provides deep assurance. But it is not the first thing people need to hear.

I remember hearing a fine talk on the resurrection which was part of a five-night series of evangelistic meetings aimed at students. A companion complained afterwards that the talk was deficient because it was not cross-centred. 'You've not preached the gospel if you've not told people that Christ died as their substitute.' I have heard similar sentiments on other occasions. But by that criterion most of the sermons of Acts would have been judged deficient and Paul would not have been invited back to speak at the next Christian Union mission! People move from the belief that atonement must be central to the Christian gospel (which is true) to believing that the mechanics of the atonement must be central to evangelistic messages (which is not true).

But this does not negate the centrality of the cross in our proclamation. Paul tells the Corinthians: 'I resolved to know nothing while I was with you except Jesus Christ and him crucified' (1 Cor. 2:2). And that must be our message as well.

2. *The word at the centre of our mission*

The priority of Jesus is proclamation because it is his word that has authority. When the word of Jesus is heard, captives are set free. This is a central theme in Luke's Gospel.

In the parable of the sower the kingdom is advanced as the seed is scattered. Jesus says the seed is 'the word of God' (Luke 8:11) and the good soil is those 'who hear the word, retain it, and by persevering produce a crop' (8:15). The true family of Jesus are those 'who hear God's word and put it into practice' (8:21). Martha is 'worried and upset about many things' (Luke 10:38-42). The word 'worried' is the same word as 'cares' in the description of rocky soil in the parable of the sower (8:14). These cares divert people from the word of God and so it is with Martha. In contrast Mary chooses 'what is better' which is to listen to Jesus' words.

In Luke 11:27-32 a woman says to Jesus that blessed is the womb that bore him. 'He replied, "Blessed rather are those who hear the word of God and obey it"' (11:28). He then responds to the request to perform a sign by saying the only sign will be the sign of Jonah. In Matthew's account it's a reference to the resurrection. But in Luke the focus is on Jonah the preacher. They want a sign, but all they get is a preacher. God's word is enough. The Queen of the South who came to hear the words of Solomon and the people of Nineveh who responded to the word preached by Jonah will condemn those who now reject that word (11:29-32).

Proclamation was central to the mission of Jesus. And proclamation is central to our mission.

After the three scenes in Luke 4, we read: 'One day as Jesus was standing by the Lake of Gennesaret, with the people crowding round him and listening to the word of God' (5:1). Jesus is teaching God's word again. So far so familiar. But then we get an extraordinary story in which Jesus tells Peter to go fishing. Peter is a fisherman and he knows there are no fish around. But now this preacher presumes to know about fishing! And sure enough they land a huge catch.

But the punch line of the story comes in verses 10-11: 'Then Jesus said to Simon, "Don't be afraid; from now on you will catch men." So they pulled their boats up on shore, left everything and followed him.' Jesus is saying, in effect, 'You've seen the power of my word – casting out of the evil spirits, healing of sickness. You've been a channel for the power as you hauled in the great catch of fish. Now I'm sending you to speak my word, to exercise my power through my word, to bring people into my kingdom.'

The word of Jesus creates a miraculous catch. Now he calls us to do the same: to rescue people through the word of Jesus.

The gospel is good news. It is news, not a lifestyle to be modelled or an ethic to be implemented or a philosophy to be debated. To be sure, it has big implications for our lifestyles, ethics and philosophies. But it is first and foremost news. It is a message to be proclaimed.

Think of the secular usage of the term. 'Gospel', as we have noted, was the term used to describe the announcement of victory in battle. Imagine a messenger bringing news from the battlefield. It is true that one would expect his behaviour to be congruent with his message. An announcement of victory from someone in mourning would create puzzlement. But he would not have announced his 'good news' of victory until words had left his mouth. It is the same for us. Our behaviour must match our message, otherwise we will create confusion. But there must be a message, otherwise we will create even greater confusion. People will assume we do good works to earn salvation.

ANNOUNCING THE RETURN OF THE KING

The climax of the ministry of Jesus in Matthew's Gospel is the Great Commission:

> Then Jesus came to them and said, 'All authority in heaven and on earth has been given to me. Therefore go and make disciples of all nations, baptising them in

the name of the Father and of the Son and of the Holy Spirit, and teaching them to obey everything I have commanded you. And surely I am with you always, to the very end of the age' (Matt. 28:18-20).

'All authority in heaven and on earth has been given to me.' This is the language of Daniel 7, which describes a vision of four beasts who represents the empires of this world. But the Ancient of Days strips them of their power and grants it instead to 'one like a son of man, coming on the clouds of heaven' (7:13): 'He was given authority, glory and sovereign power; all nations and peoples of every language worshipped him' (7:14). Jesus is the son of man of Daniel's vision who is given authority over all the nations.

The ascension of Jesus is his enthronement. In Daniel 7, the son of man does not come on the clouds to earth as Jesus will at his return (Acts 1:11). In Daniel, the son of man comes on the clouds in glory before the Ancient of Days. In other words, he enters heaven on the clouds. And this is precisely what took place at the ascension. What Luke 24:50-53 and Acts 1:9-11 depict from below, Daniel 7 depicts from above. Jesus ascends through the clouds to glory to receive all authority.

In Daniel's description of his vision, the kingdom is given to one like the son of man (7:14). But in the explanation of the vision in verse 27 the kingdom is given to the saints, to the people of God. How does that happen? What does that look like? The key is the 'therefore' in Matthew 28:18-19. It is because all authority has been given to the Son of Man that he sends us out in mission. We go to proclaim his rule. We go to call on people to submit. We go to all nations because he has been given authority over all nations. We find the same pattern in Revelation 2:26-28:

> To him who overcomes and does my will to the end, I will give authority over the nations – 'He will rule them with an iron sceptre; he will dash them to pieces like pottery' – just as I have received authority from my Father. I will also give him the morning star.

The morning star is the planet Venus. It was a Roman symbol of victory. Roman generals erected temples to the goddess Venus and carried her sign on their standards. But the Risen Christ turns all our notions of success and victory upside down. They are completely re-defined.

Verse 27 is a quote from Psalm 2. In the psalm God gives authority over the nations to his messianic King. Now Jesus says that he is giving that authority to his people. That is what happened at the Great Commission. All authority has been given to Jesus and therefore he sends us out to the nations to teach them to obey the commands of Jesus, to submit to him, to obey his rule. That is how we exercise authority over the nations. We exercise the authority of Christ not through the sword, but through the word. Or rather we exercise authority through the sword which is the word (Rev. 1:16).

The same words are quoted in Revelation 12 which tells us what it means to overcome. 'They overcame him [Satan] by the blood of the Lamb and by the word of their testimony; they did not love their lives so much as to shrink from death' (Rev. 12:10-11). How do we overcome? How do we exercise the authority of the king? By the blood of the Lamb, by the word of our testimony, by not loving our lives so much as to shrink from death. It is topsy-turvy. We rule by serving. We conquer by loving. We overcome by suffering. And it is topsy-turvy because at the heart of this vision, on the throne at the very centre of heaven, is a Lamb looking as if it has been slaughtered (Rev. 5:5-6). This is the kingdom of the crucified One. This is the empire of the Lamb.

The beasts rule. But God has taken their authority away and given it to Jesus. And so his rule spreads throughout the world through the mission of the church. We speak an authoritative word from the king. We call on men and women to submit to the Son of Man. We are given authority, the authority of the king, to extend his kingdom by proclaiming his word.

The resurrection and ascension are God's declaration that Jesus is King and as God's King he sends us to declare the coming of his kingdom to the nations, commanding people to obey his teaching. Once again God rules through his word.

It is because all authority has been given to him that Jesus sends us to all the nations. It is through the preaching of the gospel that Jesus is wielding his sceptre in the world. Even now he exercises his rule through the preaching of the gospel. Through the gospel we command people to submit to Jesus. Through the gospel judgment is passed on people who continue to reject him. To tell people the gospel is to announce the kingdom or kingship of God and his Christ.

If people acknowledge his lordship now, they will experience his coming rule as blessing, life and salvation. If they reject him, they will experience his coming rule as conquest, death and judgment.

We live in a culture where choice is everything and value judgments are relative; in which I decide what is right for me. The declaration of Christ's kingship cuts right across this. We do not invite people to make Jesus their king; we tell people that Jesus is their king. We do not invite people to meet Jesus; we warn people that they will meet Jesus as their conquering king. We do not offer people a gospel invitation; we command people to repent and submit to the coming king. Of course we do this graciously and gently (1 Pet. 3:16). We cannot force or manipulate repentance. But one day everyone will bow the knee before Jesus one way or another (Phil. 2:9-11).

Much of our evangelism takes an individual you-and-God approach: you have sinned, your sin cuts you off from God, but Jesus removes the consequences of sin so you can know God again. There is nothing incorrect about this story. But the Bible tells a much bigger, fuller story. It is the story of God creating a new humanity, reasserting his life-giving, liberating rule over the world, and bringing it to a climax in the triumph of his Son and the renewal of creation. The danger of the you-and-God message is that I remain at the centre. I am the almighty consumer, shopping around for what suits me best with God providing the best option for my religious life. God serves my spiritual needs while Tesco serves my grocery needs. And the customer is always right. An eschatological vision, by contrast, puts God firmly at the centre. The gospel tells the story of the kingdom of God. The goal of the story is the glory of God and the climax of the story is 'God all in all' (1 Cor. 15:28).

The kingdom of God extends beyond my personal concerns to encompass the renewal of all things. Here is a message of hope for those suffering injustice, inequality and abuse. Take away eschatology and life has no meaning. That is the message of Ecclesiastes. Ecclesiastes is about living in a disordered world. View the world without God – look at what is simply 'under the sun' – and the conclusion is that everything is meaningless. But the book ends with the affirmation that God will impose moral order on this world. The final verse is: 'God will bring every deed into judgment, including every hidden thing, whether it is good or evil' (Eccles. 12:14). We need to incorporate eschatology into our apologetics. We do live in a disordered world in which evil often prospers and the innocent suffer. We cannot pretend it is otherwise. But one day God will re-impose order on the world. The final judgment is the ultimate declaration that suffering matters and that evil is unacceptable. That declaration is anticipated in the cross and resurrection. The resurrection is the promise that the godlessness and godforsakenness of the cross are not the last word. God's kingdom is coming. Eternal life is coming. A new creation is coming.

The book of Acts is structured around summary statements which describe the growth of the church. Often the word of God is the agent of the sentence. 'So the word of God spread' (Acts 6:7). 'But the word of God continued to increase and spread' (Acts 12:24; 13:49; 19:20). The growth of God's kingdom is synonymous with the spread of God's word. The kingdom grows through the word as it elicits faith.

If you want to defeat your enemy in battle you surprise them. But God does not want to defeat us. And so he announces his coming. If you want to defeat your enemy you make sure they have nowhere to escape. But God does not want to defeat us. And so he provides a way of escape. He 'defeats' his own Son so that we can escape his coming.

Six

CONCLUSION: THE WHOLE COUNSEL OF GOD

THE CENTRALITY OF REPENTANCE

The Four Spiritual Laws or How to Know God Personally is the famous tract written by Bill Bright, the founder of Campus Crusade for Christ (now known in the U.S.A. as Cru). Not only is it thought to have been distributed over a billion times, but it is for many Christians the standard way in which to present the gospel. The 'four spiritual laws' which form the core of its presentation are as follows:

- God loves you and offers a wonderful plan for your life.

- Man is sinful and separate from God. Therefore, he cannot know and experience God's love and plan for his life.

- Jesus Christ is God's only provision for man's sin. Through him you can know and experience God's love and plan for your life.

- We must individually receive Jesus Christ as Saviour and Lord; then we can know and experience God's love and plan for our lives.

There is nothing false in the four spiritual laws and they have undoubtedly been used by God in the lives of millions of people.

But it is open to critique. The tract makes no mention of the Holy Spirit and places regeneration after faith. It explicitly talks about conversion as an individual act with no mention of the church nor God's intent to save a people. It makes no mention of eschatology nor God's glory, and so there is no suggestion that God's purposes extend beyond a wonderful plan for my life. On its own, this gospel will create small lives with no sense of the wider horizons of God's community, God's mission or God's glory. It does not imply the kind of radical transformation that brings you into confrontation with your culture.

Those who emphasize the gospel of the cross need to recognise the importance of the kingdom of God and the community of the kingdom, otherwise their gospel will be inadequate or incomplete. The call to repentance becomes defective if the social implications of following Christ are not made explicit.

How many of us would respond to the question, 'What must I do to find eternal life?' with a call to sell your possessions and give the money to the poor? How many of us would respond to an invitation to talk about faith in Jesus with a call to 'righteousness, self-control and judgment'? Yet these were the gospel messages of Jesus to the rich young ruler in Mark 10:17-23 and Paul to Felix in Acts 24:25. These statements were clearly context-specific. But that is the point. Jesus and Paul were spelling out the radical socio-political demands of discipleship for these two individuals.

According to some stories, soldiers during the crusades were sometimes baptized holding their swords out of the water. They didn't want the lordship of Christ to interfere with their actions in the heat of battle. We can proclaim such a privatised me-and-God gospel that the result is our watches and wallets are, in effect, held above the waters of baptism. Our politics, business and social attitudes are unaffected by the lordship of Christ.

It might help us navigate our discussion if we distinguish between the gospel itself and the implications or fruit of the gospel. The gospel describes what God does in Christ, particularly through the incarnation, death, resurrection, ascension and return of Christ. With that gospel comes a call to faith and repentance. My response is not part of the gospel itself, but it is important. The gospel has far-reaching implications for us – personal, sexual, religious, economic, social, political. We are called now to live under the lordship of Christ. But we must not confuse the gospel with its implications. Tim Keller says:

> The gospel is not about something we do but about what has been done for us, and yet the gospel results in a whole new way of life. This grace and the good deeds that result must be distinguished and connected … Just as faith and works must not be separated or confused, so the results

of the gospel must never be separated from or confused
with the gospel itself.[1]

As well as asking, 'What is the gospel?' we also need to
ask, 'What is the scope of repentance?' This might also
highlight where the real fault lines run, particular with
those whose advocacy of a cross-centred gospel actually
masks a truncated gospel.

This was the concern that drove the younger Third
World theologians like René Padilla and Samuel Escobar
at the 1974 Lausanne Congress.[2] As we have already
noted, the Congress brought together evangelicals from
across the world to plot the evangelization of the world.
But, according to John Stott, Padilla and Escobar 'set the
cat among the pigeons' at the Congress.[3] Their fear was
that the Congress would endorse an evangelistic strategy
in which, for the sake of numerical success, the claims of
the gospel would be replaced by a gospel of 'cheap grace'.
They firmly maintained that any true proclamation of the
gospel must include the call to repentance in its social as
well as individual dimensions. Escobar said:

> The temptation for evangelicals today is to reduce the
> Gospel, to mutilate it, to eliminate any demands for
> the fruit of repentance and any aspect that would make
> it unpalatable ... it must stress the need for the whole
> Gospel of Jesus Christ as Saviour and Lord whose
> demands cannot be cheapened. No eagerness for the

---

1.   Keller, *Centre Church*, 30.

2.   See Tim Chester, *Awakening to a World of Need: The Recovery of Evangelical Social Concern*, (IVP, 1993), 69-88.

3.   John Stott, *International Review of Mission*, vol. 64, no. 255 (1975), 289.

quantitative growth of the church should render us silent about the whole counsel of God.[4]

His concern arose not because he was not committed to world evangelization, but because he was. True evangelism is compromised, Escobar argued, when people, usually speaking from a position of personal affluence, undermine the very message of the gospel as they seek to make it palatable by playing down its ethical demands. 'A spirituality without discipleship in the daily social, economic and political aspects of life is religiosity and not Christianity.'[5]

The protest of Padilla and Escobar was against an easy gospel which was prepared to sacrifice the kind of discipleship demanded by the cross for the sake of numerical results. The need, they believed, was for the church to be faithful to the demands of the gospel, including in its social dimensions. The affluence of the West in contrast to the poverty of the Third World, coupled with a culturally conditioned view of the gospel and of evangelism, threatened to undermine the very cause their detractors sought to espouse – the evangelization of the world. The issue was not whether social action was part of mission, but whether the church would proclaim and adhere to a gospel that included the call to repent and to produce the fruit of good works, particularly action against poverty, racism and injustice. At Lausanne, Padilla concluded: 'The future of the church does not depend on our ability to persuade people to give intellectual assent to a truncated gospel, but on our faithfulness to the full

4.   Samuel Escobar, 'Evangelism and Man's Search for Freedom, Justice and Fulfilment,' in J. D. Douglas (Ed.), *Let the Earth Hear His Voice*, (World Wide Publications, 1975), 310.

5.   ibid., 310.

gospel of our Lord Jesus Christ and God's faithfulness to his Word.'[6]

In summary those who emphasize the gospel of the cross need to recognise that we are:

1. The ambassadors of the King – we proclaim Jesus as Lord.

2. The servants of the King – we submit our lives to Jesus as Lord.

3. The community of the King – we anticipate the consummation of his kingdom in our life together.

THE CENTRALITY OF THE CROSS

On the kingdom side of the debate, people need to recognise the centrality of the cross. Without the atonement, we have a gospel that is no gospel.

It would be pleasing to retain a symmetry in this debate. But it is asymmetrical. Without an emphasis on the kingdom, the gospel of the cross is inadequate. But without an emphasis on the cross, the gospel of the kingdom is not gospel. It becomes a gospel of good works. It may be good works to achieve the kingdom of God rather than good works to achieve personal salvation, but it is still our good works rather than the good work of Christ on our behalf. We are left with a legalistic gospel of self-righteousness through social action.

Some people have been brought up with a cross-centred emphasis and then come to discover the breadth of the kingdom. Such people can then assume the cross and emphasize the kingdom. The kingdom becomes their

---

6.   René Padilla, *Mission Between the Times*, (Eerdmans, 1985), 40.

primary emphasis. They talk about correcting one-sided theologies, but create their own one-sided theology. Nevertheless deep down there is a sense of God's grace because of their background.

But the danger is that subsequent generations simply emphasize the kingdom and social involvement. Because the gospel of grace is only assumed and not constantly drilled home it is then lost or forgotten. Human beings are all default legalists who need to be regularly pointed back to the grace of the cross.

In their book *ReJesus*, Michael Frost and Alan Hirsch claim the institutional church needs to rediscover the radical example of its Messiah – we need to 'reJesus' the church or to return to what the authors call 'radical traditionalism'. 'Our point is that to reJesus the church, we need to go back to the daring, radical, strange, wonderful, inexplicable, unstoppable, marvellous, unsettling, disturbing, caring, powerful God-Man.'[7]

The book has many strengths. There is plenty of insight and it is full of passion. Sometimes it is overstated, but then sometimes we need to be provoked. But absent are the cross and the resurrection (mentioned so infrequently they merit no inclusion in the index), and the ascension and the return of Jesus (not mentioned at all). Frost and Hirsch may be reacting against a neglect of the life of Jesus, but the answer cannot be to neglect his cross, resurrection, ascension and return.

There is a telling anecdote at the beginning of the book that encapsulates the problem.[8] The story is told of

7.   Frost and Hirsch, *ReJesus: A Wild Messiah for a Missional Church*, 111.
8.   ibid., 18.

a speaker asking an audience of 600 people with whom in the story of the healing of Jairus's daughter in Luke 8 they most identify. We are invited to be shocked that only six people identified with Jesus. But is it a mistake for people to look to Jesus as their Saviour before they look to him as their model? Do we really want lots of people with a messiah-complex?

What is missing is soteriology. Perhaps this is assumed. But it is a dangerous assumption. Christology, we are told, determines missiology which in turn determines ecclesiology. The danger is that a lifestyle shaped by the pattern of Jesus that does not arise out of gospel grace shaped by the redemption of Jesus will create a new kind of legalism – a new, edgy legalism to replace the traditional legalism, but legalism nevertheless.

Frost and Hirsch say: 'We believe that Christian faith must look to Jesus and must be well founded on him if it is to be authentic. If NASA was even 0.05 degrees off in launching a rocket to the moon, they would miss the moon by thousands of miles.'[9] It is a good point. The problem is that an attempt to reJesus the church with a cross-less, resurrection-less, ascension-less christology is surely more than a 0.05 degree misalignment.

In a previous job, I had to represent my organisation on a committee that brought together representatives of different denominations to promote social justice. The centrepiece of their activities was an annual week of awareness raising. I was the only evangelical on the committee. I attended those meetings for three or four years. Over that time it became clear to me that modernism

9.   ibid., 167.

and rationalism had stripped the faith of the other people round the table. They no longer believed in the uniqueness of Christ, the atoning work of the cross, the reality of divine judgment, the authority of Scripture. All they had left was a commitment to social justice. This was notionally based on the teachings of Christ, but in fact was heavily dependent on the values of the Enlightenment. It was no longer the gospel. It was no longer recognisable as apostolic Christianity. Most evangelical advocates of the gospel of the kingdom have not reached this point. But this is where they may be heading.

Proclaiming the whole counsel of God

When Paul said farewell to the elders of the church in Ephesus, he said this: 'I testify to you this day that I am innocent of the blood of all of you, for I did not shrink from declaring to you the whole counsel of God' (Acts 20:26-27, esv).

It is a sobering reminder of the importance of these discussions. We do not want to be guilty of the blood of people for not proclaiming the whole counsel of God. It is also a reminder that there is a fullness to proclamation that resists our urge for simplistic summaries. Don Carson comments:

> What he must mean is that he taught the burden of the whole of God's revelation, the balance of things, leaving nothing out that was of primary importance, never ducking the hard bits, helping believers to grasp the whole counsel of God that they themselves would become better equipped to read their Bibles intelligently, comprehensively. It embraced God's purposes in the history of redemption (truths to be believed and a God

to be worshiped), an unpacking of human origin, fall, redemption, and destiny (a worldview that shapes all human understanding and a Saviour without whom there is no hope), the conduct expected of God's people (commandments to be obeyed and wisdom to be pursued, both in our individual existence and in the community of the people of God), and the pledges of transforming power both in this life and in the life to come (promises to be trusted and hope to be anticipated).[10]

Part of our problem is we create reductionist gospels to aid evangelism training. We want to teach people what to say to their friends. So we create our version of the four spiritual laws – our summary of the gospel. And then we say, 'This is the gospel.' There is nothing wrong with this as a pedagogical device. The danger comes when we make these gospel summaries normative. The reality is the gospel can be summarised in the three words, 'Jesus is Lord,' as it was by Paul in Romans 10:9, and at the same time it takes the entire Bible to explain it fully.

There is a great variety to the preaching of Acts, much of which is shaped by the context in which the apostles were preaching. But, as we have already noted, the common content is this: event plus implication – the facts of the cross and resurrection plus the offer of forgiveness. The links between the two (union with Christ, substitutionary atonement and justification by faith) are developed in the Epistles and are foundational to orthodoxy. But they need not be part of our initial proclamation.

---

10. D. A. Carson, 'Challenges for the Twenty-First-Century Pulpit,' in Leland Ryken and Todd Wilson (Eds), *Preach the Word: Essays on Expository Preaching: In Honour of R. Kent Hughes*, (Crossway, 2007), 177-178.

But neither are union with Christ, substitutionary atonement and justification by faith peripheral. A church which does not affirm these things is heading for disaster. The polarity between Jesus and Paul or between the Gospels and the Epistles is a false polarity. The contrast is not between Jesus and Paul, but simply between one type of apostolic writing and another. In other words, the differences are literary rather than theological.

The key issue is this: We have no Christ other than the Christ presented to us by the apostles. This is the point of 1 John. 1 John is written to reassure the members of a church after some leading figures have left them. They have left a particular local church, claiming to follow a superior version of Christianity. But John says they went out from 'us' (in contrast to 'you', his readers). 'They went out from us, but they did not really belong to us. For if they had belonged to us, they would have remained with us; but their going showed that none of them belonged to us. But you have an anointing from the Holy One, and all of you know the truth' (1 John 2:19-20).

The 'us' here are the apostles (as 1:1-4 makes clear). The reason these people left the church is actually that they have left apostolic Christianity. And to leave apostolic Christianity, says John, is to leave the truth (2:20-27). Why? Because the apostles were the ones who heard and saw and touched Jesus – as John repeatedly emphasizes in 1:1-4.

Not only were they eye-witnesses of Jesus, but Jesus gave them the Holy Spirit to testify to the truth about Jesus so that the apostolic testimony would be accurate (John 15:26-27; 16:12-15). Paul's inclusion among the apostles was always going to be controversial, but that issue was resolved during his lifetime, nearly 2,000 years ago.

God revealed himself in Jesus, the Word-made-flesh. How do we have access to that revelation? Through the testimony of the apostles who heard and saw and touched Jesus. How do we have access to the apostolic testimony? In the Spirit-inspired writings of the New Testament. To pit Jesus against Paul is to claim to have a better or equal grasp of the person of Christ than the Spirit-inspired eye-witnesses.

Part of the problem is that people often dip into the Gospels to examine isolated stories rather than trace the plotline of the Gospels which lead you inexorably to the cross and resurrection. As it happens, the synthesis between cross and kingdom outlined in this book has focused on the Gospels. When the Gospels are taken seriously as literary wholes, then the differences between their message and that of the Epistles diminish.

THE WHOLE COUNSEL OF GOD IN A
MISSIONAL CONTEXT

The fact is that any discussion of the essential elements of the gospel seems far removed from the realities of mission in a post-Christian context. We can no longer assume that the people we are trying to teach share a biblical worldview. It is therefore rare for someone to hear the gospel message and immediately decide to turn to Christ in faith and repentance. Conversion for most people with little Christian background is usually a process, albeit one which may have some decisive moments. Paul's ministry in Ephesus, for example, took place over at least two years (Acts 19:10). This is the context in which he taught the whole counsel of God.

In this type of situation a person's knowledge of the gospel is built up through multiple encounters with the truth. Some of those may take the form of gospel presentations. Some may be snatches of conversations with Christian friends. In this kind of context the extent of the content of any one presentation or conversation is less critical. But over time we want, as Carson puts it in the above quotation, to teach 'the burden of the whole of God's revelation, the balance of things, leaving nothing out that was of primary importance, never ducking the hard bits'. We will proclaim the good news of God's coming reign of justice, peace and joy, anticipated now, as individuals submit to the lordship of Christ and anticipated in the communal life of the church. And we will proclaim the good news that the King dies in our place on the cross so that those who by faith are in him can enjoy his coming reign as justice, peace and joy.

PORTERBROOK NETWORK
Is all about biblical training for mission and ministry, where you are, through our book series and two curriculums:
- – Porterbrook Learning
- – Porterbrook Seminary

PORTERBROOK LEARNING
Porterbrook Learning is an online training curriculum, for equipping Christians for ministry in the local church and church planting. It connects the heart and mission to the Bible story.

24 online modules to choose from covering:
- Bible and Doctrine
- Character
- Church
- World

PORTERBROOK SEMINARY
Porterbrook Seminary allows you to study in-depth in the context of your ministry over 3 years. Get input from world-class theologians and pastor-practitioners that will shape your ministry.
- For leaders and planters to train in the context of ministry
- An affordable and flexible college level course that prepares people for leadership in local church ministries
- 3 years (or study a year at a time), 10 hours study a week, 3 residentials and 7 assignments a year

For more information visit www.porterbrooknetwork.org

Christian Focus Publications

Our mission statement –

STAYING FAITHFUL
In dependence upon God we seek to impact the world through literature faithful to His infallible Word, the Bible. Our aim is to ensure that the Lord Jesus Christ is presented as the only hope to obtain forgiveness of sin, live a useful life and look forward to heaven with Him.

Our books are published in four imprints:

CHRISTIAN
FOCUS

Popular works including biographies, commentaries, basic doctrine and Christian living.

CHRISTIAN
HERITAGE

Books representing some of the best material from the rich heritage of the church.

MENTOR

Books written at a level suitable for Bible College and seminary students, pastors, and other serious readers. The imprint includes commentaries, doctrinal studies, examination of current issues and church history.

CF4•K

Children's books for quality Bible teaching and for all age groups: Sunday school curriculum, puzzle and activity books; personal and family devotional titles, biographies and inspirational stories – Because you are never too young to know Jesus!

Christian Focus Publications Ltd,
Geanies House, Fearn, Ross-shire,
IV20 1TW, Scotland, United Kingdom.
www.christianfocus.com